Elizabeth Bishop

A Bibliography

1927-1979

Elizabeth Bishop

A Bibliography

1927-1979

Candace W. MacMahon

Published for the Bibliographical Society of
the University of Virginia

by the University Press of Virginia
Charlottesville

A Linton R. Massey Descriptive Bibliography

THE UNIVERSITY PRESS OF VIRGINIA
Copyright © 1980 by the Rector and Visitors
of the University of Virginia

First published 1980

Library of Congress Cataloging in Publication Data
MacMahon, Candace W
    Elizabeth Bishop: a bibliography, 1927–1979
    "A Linton R. Massey descriptive bibliography."
    Includes index.
    1. Bishop, Elizabeth, 1911–1979—Bibliography.
I. Virginia. University. Bibliographical Society.
Z8098.9.M34   [PS3503.I785]   016.811′5′4   79–13063
ISBN 0-8139-0783-7

Printed in the United States of America

For Dr. Anny Baumann

Contents

Foreword

Upon being "bibliographed," as Edmund Wilson put it, I find I am suffering from "mixty motions," as a student's paper put *that*. I am rather pleased to see I've written so much when I've always thought I'd written so little; on the other hand, I am rather appalled by how bad some of the things I've written actually are. Also, between every item on Mrs. MacMahon's list, it pains me to think that there should be two or three more, and better, items to be listed. Perhaps the one advantage of being bibliographed while still alive is just that: after all, one can tell oneself hopefully, like John Paul Jones, "I have not yet begun to fight." I thank Candace MacMahon for the hard work she has done on this book, and if it has that effect on me I shall be even more grateful.

I don't imagine that bibliographies go into second editions very often, so if I ever discover (or remember) where an early poem of mine titled "Wading at Wellfleet" was first published, I shall let her know immediately, and perhaps that important (to people who read bibliographies) fact can be pasted in this book.

ELIZABETH BISHOP

Acknowledgments

This book had reached galleys when Elizabeth Bishop died on October 6, 1979. Without her invaluable cooperation certain items would never have been found and some mistakes would not have been corrected. In addition to those contributions for which she is credited elsewhere in this book, she graciously identified unsigned pieces and gave me clues which led to the location of entries which I could not have found without her help. Most of all, I am grateful for her patience, her active concern with exactness, and for her time, especially the time she took to decipher Xerox specimens of her own handwriting and to correct my mistakes. I need not add that I am supremely grateful for her literary accomplishments which form the occasion and basis for this work. I regret that she will not see it completed.

I began compiling entries in September 1975 under the direction of Professor J. D. Thomas at Rice University, later to learn that Professor Lloyd Schwartz of Boston College had completed a bibliography of Elizabeth Bishop in the form of a checklist as part of his dissertation at Harvard University in November 1975, the use of which Professor Schwartz had chosen to restrict. I wish to thank Professor Schwartz for his cooperation and help once we discovered our mutual interest in the works of Elizabeth Bishop. Specifically, I wish to thank him for the following contributions: **B15, Bb6, C86, C127, C152, C153, C154, J17, J18, J28, N22, N25,** and **Appendix I6.**

Professor Fredson Bowers of the University of Virginia is also most deserving of my appreciation for his careful attention to the text and for the time he spent making helpful suggestions concerning changes and revisions. I am also most grateful to Professor Irvin Ehrenpreis, my first reader, for his recommendations and corrections.

I am greatly indebted to George Bixby, of Ampersand Books, who offered me his knowledge and support throughout this project and who kindly loaned part of his collection to be photographed. Robert Wilson, of the Phoenix Book Shop, contributed significantly to Section B and the translations.

The staffs of Miss Bishop's publishers—Farrar, Straus and Giroux; Houghton Mifflin; Victor Gollancz; Wesleyan; Chatto & Windus; and The Ecco Press—were very kind about supplying information about her books. I am indebted to Cynthia Krupat for typographical information.

Special thanks are owed to Clive E. Driver and Patricia C. Willis of the Rosenbach Foundation for their invaluable assistance as well as their permission to publish the excerpts from Miss Bishop's letters to Marianne Moore. I am also grateful to Rodney G. Dennis, of the Houghton Library, Harvard University, who supplied the letters from Houghton Mifflin. Abstracts from these letters between Houghton Mifflin Company and Elizabeth Bishop are reprinted by permission of Houghton Mifflin Company, Boston, and by permission of the Houghton Library. Title and copyright pages of Miss Bishop's books are reproduced with the permission of Farrar, Straus and Giroux, Inc.

It is impossible to acknowledge everyone who has helped me. Omissions here as in the bibliography are unintentional. I am grateful to and for all the following people who offered me assistance, often multiple times, and in some cases daily: Richard Perrine, Fern Hyman, Charles Goodson, and the rest of the staff of the Fondren Library, Rice University, where most of this work was prepared; Bobby Cook of the Houston Public Library; the staff of the Widener Library, Harvard University; the staff of the Humanities Research Department, the University of Texas at Austin; the staff of the New York Public Library; the staff of the Vassar College Library; Professor Craig S. Abbott, of Northern Illinois University; Samuel Bachrach, M.D., of the Worcester County Poetry Association; Anny Baumann, M.D., who introduced me to Elizabeth Bishop's work; Frank Bidart; Dorothy Bowie; Andreas Brown, of the Gotham Book Mart; Professor Ashley Brown, of the University of South Carolina, for three Brazilian interviews (Q1, Q4, Q9); John Ciardi; Kit Clark for her typing; Mrs. Louis Henry Cohn, of House of Books, Ltd.; Leslie Dear, of Random House, for publication information; Herman Detering and Oscar Graham, of Detering Book Gallery, who advertised for my books; Deborah E. Drake, of Harper's Bazaar; J. M. Edelstein, for his assistance and suggestions; Professor Sybil Estess, of the University of Houston; Holly Hall, of the James M. Olin Library, Washington University; Mary Haynes, for her editing; John Hollander; Peter Howard, of Serendipity Books, Berkeley, California; Richard Howard; David Ishii; Professor Ivar Ivask, of *World Literature Today*, who wrote me many letters; Professor Robert C. Jones, of Central Missouri State; Karl Killian, of the Brazos Bookstore,

Houston, Texas; S. Kroupa, Special Collections, University of Washington Libraries; Herbert Leibowitz, of *Parnassus: Poetry in Review*; Norman E. Lovely, of the Worcester Public Library; Michele Medinz, of the Viking Press, for publication information; Howard Moss; Professor John Meixner, of Rice University; Julian and Edith Nangle, of Words Etcetera, London, for their catalogues; Professor Jane C. Nitzsche, of Rice University, who examined the English deposit copies; Professor William B. Piper, Rice University; Father William Sheehan, of the Woodstock Theological Library, Georgetown University, who gathered information at the Library of Congress; Claes Sjorgreen, of Charles Scribner's Sons, for publication information; Louisa Solana, of the Grolier Book Shop, Cambridge, Massachusetts; Donald Stanford, of the *Southern Review*; Nancy Steeper, of Friends of the Smith College Library; Christopher Stephens, of Canfield and Stephens; Karen Swenson; May Swenson; Dean Louis Swilley; Professor Joy Wilson, of the University of St. Thomas, Houston, Texas; Professor Geoff Winningham, of Rice University, for doing the photographs; A. J. van der Staay, of the Rotterdam Arts Council, for the information on Poetry International; and Professor Christine VanBoheemen, of the University of Leiden, who translated the Dutch articles for me.

Finally, I must confess that neither Professor Schwartz nor I, even with the kind assistance of Miss Bishop, have found an early poem, "Wading at Wellfleet," in any of the periodicals acknowledged in *North & South* or in any other publication prior to its appearance in her first book. Miss Bishop, however, insisted that it was published somewhere in 1939. This is the most important of several mysteries, which include two missing Japanese translations and a Miami interview, all of which Miss Bishop recalled, but which we did not locate.

C. W. M.

Rice University

Bibliographical Method

Section A lists chronologically descriptions of the first printings, cloth and paper, of all trade editions, American and English, of Elizabeth Bishop's separate publications, including one she translated, one she wrote with the Editors of *Life*, and one she edited with Emanuel Brasil. I have quoted all relevant dust jacket and paperback wrapper information in full. The photographs of the copyright pages have been compacted wherever possible to omit blank space.

Here I also describe two proof copies, *The Complete Poems* (Farrar, Straus and Giroux) and *The Diary of "Helena Morley"* (Ecco Press). These are the only sets of bound galleys that I have located. Although it has become policy for Farrar, Straus and Giroux to issue such galleys for all new books, it would seem that *Questions of Travel* was printed before this practice was established, and *Geography III* was rushed to print so late in the year that this stage of the production process was skipped. The publisher can give me no information about the possible existence of these galleys, for they keep no record of them. There may be other proof copies for the English editions; I have not seen them.

Numbering of Entries: A2.a3 is the first paperback impression of *Poems: North & South—A Cold Spring*. A refers to the section, 2 indicates that it is Miss Bishop's second book, a denotes a specific publisher's edition, and 3 is the number of the impression designated by the publisher. The change of binding to paper is not indicated in the numbering.

In the case of such items as A4.[c1], the brackets are used to indicate that the trade designation of this printing as the first impression of a new edition is not the correct bibliographical description, for although this is the first English impression, it is technically the first edition, third impression, as is explained in parentheses following the title. An asterisk following these numbers indicates a proof copy, a set of bound galleys, as in the case of A4.[b1]* *The Diary of "Helena Morley"*, The Ecco Press, [1977].

At the first appearance of a poem (which may occur in Section A, B, or C) both subsequent printings and variants are listed if either occurred. Subsequent printings are designated by sigla (see Abbreviations list); the sigla of American and English printings are separated by a solidus (/). Miss Bishop did not see proofs for any English books; therefore recorded variants are noted only for subsequent American printings, and not for reprintings in anthologies.

For changes within lines, I give the line number and the original word or words followed by a bracket, the variant and the sigla for all printings in which it has appeared or the first printing followed by a plus (+) indicating that it appears in all subsequent printings. A wavy dash (~) represents the same word or phrase that appears before the bracket. An inferior caret ($_\wedge$) indicates the absence of a punctuation mark when a difference in the punctuation constitutes the variant being recorded or is a part of the variant. A vertical stroke (|) represents a line ending. A double vertical stroke (||) represents additional intervening line spacing between lines.

Copy Locations: Copy location symbols are those given in the *National Union Catalog* and those designed to supplement it:

BL: British Library
CWM: Collection of compiler
DeU: University of Delaware, Newark
DLC: Library of Congress
EB: Elizabeth Bishop
MoSW: Washington University, St. Louis, Missouri
TxR: Rice University, Houston, Texas
TxU: University of Texas at Austin
ViU: University of Virginia, Charlottesville

Letters: The excerpted passages of letters following items **A1** and **A2** are from the correspondence between Miss Bishop and Houghton Mifflin, now in the Houghton Library, Harvard University. They reflect the bibliographical history of the books. I decided to use these after studying J. M. Edelstein's *Wallace Stevens: A Descriptive Bibliography* (Pittsburgh: University of Pittsburgh Press, 1973). One unintentional spelling error has been silently corrected.

Section B lists chronologically brief descriptions of books that include a contribution by Miss Bishop appearing for the first time in a book. Here, in subsection Bb, I include Miss Bishop's comments on dust jackets because they are not large enough to constitute a section and were written, with the possible exception of the one on *O to Be a Dragon*, specifically as comments for these books.

Section C lists chronologically Miss Bishop's contributions to periodicals. When an original typescript is available to the public, its location is noted. The passages that begin "EB to MM" are from letters of Elizabeth Bishop to Marianne Moore, now in the Marianne Moore Collection of the Rosenbach Museum in Philadelphia. Unintentional spelling errors have been silently corrected.

Section D lists translations of Miss Bishop's works, arranged alphabetically by language and then under the following categories: Mimeographed Sheets, Anthologies, Periodicals, and Books.

Section E lists chronologically phonorecordings of Miss Bishop reading her work.

Section F lists chronologically musical settings.

Section G consists of the only book-length study of Elizabeth Bishop.

Section H lists alphabetically by author the contributions in a journal issue devoted to Elizabeth Bishop.

Section I lists alphabetically by author books partially about Elizabeth Bishop.

Section J lists alphabetically by author articles in periodicals about or containing information on Elizabeth Bishop and her work.

Section K lists reviews alphabetically by author. Certain shorter reviews appearing in *Booklist*, *Kirkus Reviews*, *Library Journal*, *Publisher's Weekly*, and *Young Reader's Review* have been omitted. Only when an abstract of a review in one of these has been printed in *Book Review Digest* is the review listed, together with the reference information for the abstract.

Section L lists alphabetically by title continuing sources of updated biography.

Section M lists notices of awards chronologically.

Section N lists alphabetically by author various works that mention Elizabeth Bishop.

Section O lists chronologically poems dedicated to or mentioning Elizabeth Bishop.

Section P lists alphabetically by title anthologies, excluding those in Section B, in which Elizabeth Bishop's works are represented. These titles are not first appearances.

Section Q lists chronologically interviews.

Section R lists chronologically published letters and excerpts from letters of Elizabeth Bishop.

Section S lists chronologically obituaries.

Section T lists addenda.

Appendix I lists unpublished poems chronologically.

Appendix II describes an unauthorized broadside.

Chronology of Books and Awards

1945   Houghton Mifflin Poetry Award
1946   *North & South*
1947   Guggenheim Fellowship
1949–50 Consultant in Poetry, Library of Congress, Washington,
        D.C.
1951   American Academy of Arts and Letters Award
        First Lucy Martin Donnelly Fellowship from Bryn Mawr
        College
1952   Shelley Memorial Award
1954   Life Membership, National Institute of Arts and Letters
1955   *Poems: North & South—A Cold Spring*
1956   Partisan Review Fellowship
        Pulitzer Prize for Poetry
        Poems, London
1957   *The Diary of "Helena Morley"*
        Amy Lowell Traveling Fellowship
1962   Chapelbrook Fellowship
        Brazil
1964   Fellowship of the Academy of American Poets Award
1965   *Questions of Travel*
1966–67 Rockefeller Foundation Grant
        Selected Poems, London
1968   *The Ballad of the Burglar of Babylon*
        LL.D., Smith College
1969   *The Complete Poems*
        Merrill Foundation Award
1970   *The Complete Poems*, London
        National Book Award
        Order of Rio Branco (Brazil)
1972   *An Anthology of Twentieth-Century Brazilian Poetry*
        LL.D., Rutgers University
        LL.D., Brown University
1973   *Poem*

1974   Harriett Monroe Award
1975   St. Botolph Club Arts Award
1976   Books Abroad / Neustadt International Prize for Literature
        Membership, American Academy of Arts and Letters
        Geography III
        National Book Critics Circle Poetry Award
1977   LL.D., Adelphi University
1978   LL.D., Brandeis University
        Guggenheim Fellowship
1979   LL.D., Dalhousie University
        LL.D., Princeton University

Abbreviations

ALLC   *A Library of Literary Criticism: Modern American Litera-*
            ture. Dorothy Nyren Curley, Coordinator. New York:
            Fredrick Ungar Publishing Company, 1969.
An   *An Anthology of Twentieth-Century Brazilian Poetry*
ATCL   *Articles on Twentieth Century Literature.* New York:
            Kraus-Thompson Organization, 1973.
BRD   *Book Review Digest.* New York: The Wilson Company.
CLC   *Contemporary Literary Criticism.* Detroit: Gale Research
            Company.
CS   *A Cold Spring*
CP   *Complete Poems*
EB   Elizabeth Bishop
FSG   Farrar, Straus and Giroux
GIII   *Geography III*
HM (AO)   Houghton Mifflin (Austin G. Olney)
HM (FG)   Houghton Mifflin (Ferris Greenslet)
HM (JP)   Houghton Mifflin (Jean Pedrick)
HM (NG)   Houghton Mifflin (Natalie Green)
HM (PB)   Houghton Mifflin (Paul Brooks)
MM   Marianne Moore
NBCC   National Book Critics Circle
NS   *North & South*
P   *Poems* (Chatto and Windus)
Po   *Poems: North & South—A Cold Spring*
QT   *Questions of Travel*
S   *Selected Poems*

A

Separate Publications

A1 *North & South*. Houghton Mifflin, Boston, 1946 (first edition, first impression)

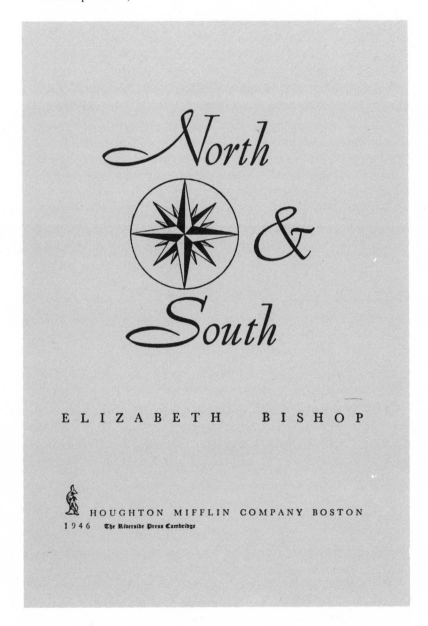

Title Page: 8¹⁵⁄₁₆ × 5¹³⁄₁₆ in. (226 × 148 mm.). Compass rose printed in deep Blue (Centroid 179).

*Acknowledgments are due to: Partisan Review, The New Yorker,
The New Republic, Direction, New Directions, New Democracy,
Life & Letters To-day, Poetry, A Magazine of Verse, The Forum,
Harper's Bazaar.*

Most of these poems were written, or partly written, before 1942.

The Riverside Press
CAMBRIDGE · MASSACHUSETTS
PRINTED IN THE U.S.A.

Collation: [unsigned 1–4⁸]; 32 leaves; [i–iv] v [vi–viii], 1–54 [55–56].

Contents: p. i: half title: 'N | [compass rose] & | S'; p. ii: 'North &
South | Winner of Tenth Anniversary | Houghton Mifflin Fellowship
Award | For a Volume of Poetry'; p. iii: title page; p. iv: copyright page;
pp. v–vi: 'Contents'; p. vii: half title; p. viii: blank; pp. 1–54: text; pp.
55–56: blank.

Typography: text 11/14 Baskerville; display: created for this book; type
page measures 174 × 105 mm., 36 lines per page; a double rule divides
the title of each poem from the text.

Paper and Binding: leaf measures 8¹⁵⁄₁₆ × 5¹⁵⁄₁₆ in. (226 × 151 mm.);
yWhite (Centroid 92) wove paper; top edges trimmed; fore and bottom
edges rough trimmed; yWhite wove endpapers; unglazed d. Blue (183)
cloth cover measures 9¼ × 6¼ in. (233 × 156 mm); front cover: in
silver, '[centered, upper half] *North & South* | [right of center, lower

half, compass rose]'; spine: vertical, in silver, '*North & South* [compass needle] Bishop H.M. Co.'

Dust Jacket, by Samuel Hanks Bryant: front: on a background of l. greenish Gray (154) streaked with grayish Green (150), '[gy.G] *North* | *&* | [deep Red (13)] *South* | [White (263)] BY ELIZABETH BISHOP | *Winner of the Houghton Mifflin Poetry Award*'; spine: vertical, '[on greenish Gray (155.5), in yWhite (92)] *North & South* BISHOP [in l. Gray (264)] *Houghton Mifflin Co.*'; back: on yWhite, in v.d. Green (147), 'North & South *By Elizabeth Bishop* | Selected unanimously as the winner of the Houghton Mifflin Company | Poetry Prize Fellowship Contest in 1945, NORTH & SOUTH is | Miss Bishop's first collection to appear between covers. It is the work | of a poet with a high ironic intelligence, verbal magic, and subtle | melody. The publishers are proud to introduce Miss Bishop in a book | form on the same list that has presented H.D., Archibald MacLeish, | and Amy Lowell. $2.00 || FREEDOM'S FARM *By Josephine Young Case* | [description, 7 lines of type] || DOCTOR JOHNSON'S WATER-FALL | *By Helen Bevington* | [description, 8 lines of type] || THE FAULTLESS SHORE *By Edward Weismiller* | [description, 7 lines of type]'; front flap: White, in v.d.G, '$2.00 | North | & [compass rose] | South | By Elizabeth Bishop | [¶] Out of more than eight hun-|dred poetry manuscripts submitted in | Houghton Mifflin Com-pany's Poetry | Prize Fellowship Contest in 1945, | NORTH & SOUTH was the unani-|mous and enthusiastic selection of the | three judges. | [¶] Miss Bishop's poetry first appeared | in print in 1935 in the important an-|thology of poetry, "Trial Balances." Since then she has published in *New* | *Directions, The New Yorker, Partisan Re-|view*, and similar periodicals. Her work | has been recognized as serious and of | great promise. Its publication has | been solicited by numerous leading | publishers, but NORTH & SOUTH | will be her first collection to appear | between covers. It is the work of a | poet with a high ironic intelligence, | verbal magic, and subtle melody. | [¶] In the poetry number of *The Satur-|day Review of Literature*, in the leading | article on meaning in modern poetry, | the writer considers Miss Bishop as | one of the most typical of truly modern | poets. Her work, he says, is an ex-|ample of the new attitude of man to-|wards himself and his world. | [¶] The publishers are proud to be the | first to introduce Miss Bishop in book | form to the American poetry-reading | public on the same list that has | presented H. D., Archibald MacLeish, | and

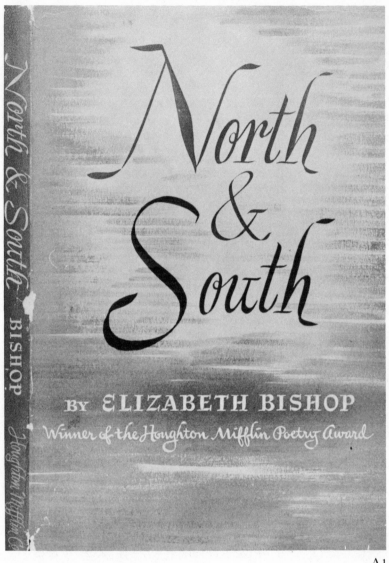

A1

Amy Lowell. ‖ *Jacket by Samuel Hanks Bryant*'; back flap: description of *Freedom's Farm*, 40 lines of type.

Text Contents: "The Map," "The Imaginary Iceberg," "Casabianca," "The Colder the Air," "Wading at Wellfleet," "Chemin de Fer," "The Gentleman of Shalott," "Large Bad Picture," "From the Country to the City," "The Man-Moth," "Love Lies Sleeping," "A Miracle for Breakfast," "The Weed," "The Unbeliever," "The Monument,"

"Paris, 7A.M.," "Quai d'Orleans," "Sleeping on the Ceiling," "Sleeping Standing Up," "Cirque d'Hiver," "Florida," "Jerónimo's House," "Roosters," "Seascape," "Little Exercise," "The Fish," "Late Air," "Cootchie," "Songs for a Colored Singer," "Anaphora."

Publication: first printing: 1,000 copies published on August 20, 1946, at $2.00; second printing: 500 copies, 1946 (in cloth); third printing: 250 copies, 1948 (in cloth).

Locations: CWM, DLC, EB, MoSW (with dust jacket), TxR, TxU.
Note: MoSW has recently acquired a set of publisher's page proofs which differs in content and arrangement from the printed version.

First Appearance: "Wading at Wellfleet"   NS, Po, CP / P
18   way,]   ~; CP

Note: According to the letters now on file in the Houghton Library, Houghton Mifflin originally solicited the manuscript.
HM (JP) to EB, November 22, 1944: We were very much interested here to read your group of poems, "Songs for a Colored Singer" in the fall issue of the Partisan Review. There is a fresh quality in the songs, and I think a superb bringing together of the tragic and the humorous in the way life so often brings them together, and poets so seldom do. The things sort of stick in the mind and go on singing themselves there. [¶] We are enclosing a blank for the new poetry award we are giving this year along with our regular annual fellowships, and we sincerely hope for an opportunity to consider your splendid work.
EB to HM (JP), December 8, 1944: Thank you very much for your kind letter about my poems, "Songs for a Colored Singer," in the fall Partisan Review, and for asking me to submit my work for your annual fellowship.
EB to HM (FG), January 11, 1946: All I had in mind about format was this: I dislike the modern unglazed linen bindings so very much that I wondered if I could have a glazed one? And could it be dark grey? I think that quite a dark gray with a gilt "NORTH & SOUTH" down the back would look nice, don't you?—and if gilt is not possible maybe a dark blue lettering? Looking over the mms. as a whole it seems to me a slightly squarer than usual book would suit it—but I don't know how large you intend to make it and it would all depend on that. Is there any possibility that I can have something to say about the type?
HM (FG) to EB, January 18, 1946: There is one poem and only one

that seems to have no title, the one beginning "From a magician's midnight sleeve". Have you anything in mind for it?

EB to HM (FG), January 22, 1945 [1946]: Yes, there is a type that I especially like for poetry—Baskerville. I think that Baskerville monotype, 169E, makes the best looking poetry pages I've seen printed. I particularly dislike those light type faces some publishers seem to think appropriate for poetry. It seems to me that the Baskerville monotype 169 E, 11 point, would be perfect—but 11 point might be too big—it might make too many run-over lines—maybe they could try and see. It would all depend on the size of the page. [¶] I have one more request. Don't you think the title would look well as "NORTH & SOUTH", using the "&" sign? It seems more forceful that way to me. Maybe after a while they could send me a title-page to brood over—as you see, I guess, I am very much interested in typography. [¶] I have another idea that I think you will agree with. The fact that none of these poems deal directly with the war, at a time when so much war poetry is being published, will, I am afraid, leave me open to reproach. The chief reason is simply that I work very slowly. But I think it would help some if a note to the effect that most of the poems had been written, or begun at least, before 1941, could be inserted at the beginning, say just after the acknowledgments. I'll enclose a sheet with the acknowledgments and such a note, to see what you think.

HM (FG) to EB, January 23, 1946: I have always liked Baskerville myself, and we used to use it frequently for special books in the good old days before the paper shortage. I will pass the suggestion along to the production department in your own words, also the sound idea of using the ampersand symbol in the title. The prefatory note is well conceived.

EB to HM (FG), April 26, 1946: I have just looked through the various books of poetry in my bookcase and find that with one exception the page numbers are all *without* brackets. I don't know quite what to make of this except that it obviously can be done. Even more important from the point of view of appearance was the lack of space between the numbers and the last lines—they looked very cramped, at least in those two sample pages.you sent me.

EB to HM (FG), April 29, 1946: I have left out one poem that seemed to be too slight when put with the others and it will also mean leaving out the acknowledgment to *Harper's Bazaar* in the list of acknowledgments.

HM (FG) to EB, April 30, 1946: This is in reply to your letters of the 26th and the 29th. We have labored with our printers, and they are going to take a chance on leaving the brackets off the figures at the bottom of the pages. I judge that you have or will indicate in the proof the omission of the poem you speak of and the acknowledgment of it in the list of such.

EB to HM (FG), June 4, 1946: In the first stanza, line seven, of THE IMAGINARY ICEBERG, the word should be *ship's*, singular, instead of *ships'* as it is printed.

HM (AO) to EB, June 19, 1946: . . . I have showed your note of June 4th to the Production Dept. Their verdict is that it is too late to change the first printing but a corrigendum has been issued for a second printing.

EB to HM (NG), July 8, 1946: Mr. Greenslet also told me to begin with that I would receive page proofs. Later this was changed but again I don't see any reason why I shouldn't now that there is more time. I also was to receive a *sample* dust jacket, and cover. I haven't received any cover at all and the dust jacket was recently sent to me already printed and is a great disappointment. I suppose nothing further can be done about that but I don't understand why things are done in this manner. [¶] The most important thing of all however is that I should like to be given an opportunity to see what you are going to print in the way of blurbs on the jacket before they are irrevocable. Quite a while ago Mr. Greenslet sent me some such material and I partially re-wrote it at his suggestion. It was so full of mistakes and wrong emphasis that it makes me very nervous to think what may appear on the dust-jacket. Will you please let me know about this?

HM (FG) to EB, July 12, 1946: Perhaps the blurbs are not quite as you would have liked them best, but we have followed your suggestions apropos of the copy that was sent you some time ago. In any case, I don't think critical readers pay much attention to publisher's jacket an-nouncements. [¶] I had this morning an hour's talk with T. S. Eliot and told him quite a lot about NORTH & SOUTH, for which he expressed a very keen interest and asked to have a copy sent him at the earliest possible moment. This might perhaps lead to its being handled in England by his own publishers, Faber and Faber, for whom he is also a very active director. In any case, it might bring us a very useful opinion.

HM (PB) to EB, August 22, 1946: Pre-publication sales of *North and South* amounted to approximately 900 copies. This, as you probably know, is a good representation for a book of poems. I am eagerly awaiting the reviews. [¶] You doubtless saw our initial advertising in the *Times* and *Herald Tribune*.

A2 *Poems: North & South—A Cold Spring*. Houghton Mifflin, Boston, 1955 (first edition, first impression)

Poems

NORTH & SOUTH—A COLD SPRING

BY ELIZABETH BISHOP

HOUGHTON MIFFLIN COMPANY BOSTON

The Riverside Press Cambridge

1955

Title Page: 8⅜ × 5⅝ in. (212 × 142 mm.).

Collation: [unsigned 1–3⁸ 4⁴ 5–7⁸]; 52 leaves; [i–iv] v [vi] vii–viii, [1–2] 3–56 [57–60] 61–95 [96].

Contents: p. i: half title: 'Poems'; p. ii: blank; p. iii: title page; p. iv: copyright page; p. v: 'Acknowledgments'; p. vi: blank; pp. vii–viii: 'Contents'; p. 1: 'North & South'; p. 2: blank; pp. 3–56: text; p. 57: 'A Cold Spring' and 6 lines of acknowledgments; p. 58: blank; p. 59: dedication: *'To Dr. Anny Baumann'*; p. 60: blank; pp. 61–95: text; p. 96: blank.

Typography: text: 11/16 Janson; display: Deepdene; type page measures 169 × 101 mm., 36 lines per page.

Paper and Binding: leaf measures 8⅜ × 5⅝ in. (212 × 142 mm.); yWhite (Centroid 92) wove paper; top edges trimmed and stained brill. Yellow Green (116); fore edges rough trimmed; bottom edges trimmed; yWhite wove endpapers; glazed m. Blue (182) cloth cover measures 8⅝ × 5⅞ in. (217 × 149 mm.); front cover: in White (263), 'Poems'; spine: in White, '[vertical] Poems | [horizontal] H. M. Co. | [vertical] Bishop'.

Dust Jacket, by Loren McIver: l. Blue (181) and White (263) with a brill. Yellow Green (116) leaf, front and back; front: all on a brill. YG leaf in typewriter type, 'P O E M S | North & South | A Cold Spring | ELIZABETH BISHOP'; spine: vertical, Black (267) typewriter type, on White, 'P O E M S Elizabeth Bishop H. M. Co.'; back, design of brill. YG leaf on l.B and White background, reverse of front without type; front flap: Black typewriter type on l.B, '$3.50 | P O E M S | North & South — | A Cold Spring | BY ELIZABETH BISHOP |

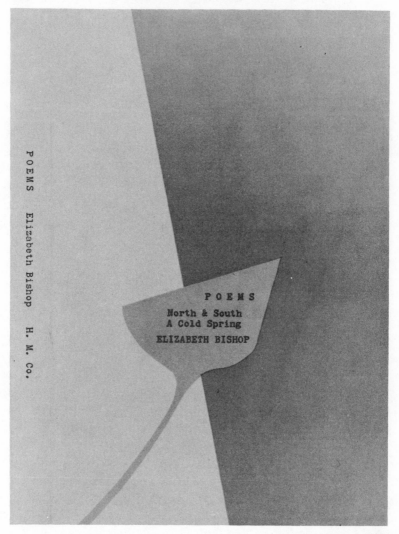

POEMS Elizabeth Bishop H. M. Co.

POEMS
North & South
A Cold Spring
ELIZABETH BISHOP

A2

[¶] This volume represents the | collected poems of an important | American poet, Elizabeth Bishop. | Her first book North & South, won | the Houghton Mifflin Company | Poetry Award and seldom has a new | collection of poems been greeted | with such critical enthusiasm. | [¶] "At last," wrote Marianne Moore | in The Nation, "we have a prize | book that has no creditable | mannerisms. At last we have some-|one who knows, who is not | didactic." Reviewing the poems for | The New Yorker, Louise Bogan | wrote, "They strike no attitudes

| and have not an ounce of super-|fluous emotional weight, and they | combine an unforced ironic humor | with a naturalist's accuracy of | observation, for Miss Bishop, | although she frequently writes | fantasy, is firmly in touch with | the real world and takes a | Thoreau-like interest in whatever | catches her attention." And in | <u>Furioso</u> Arthur Mizener said, "It | is easy to say that these poems | are well worth having waited for; | they are. It is not easy to say | why, to say honestly how they use, | without abusing, the rhetorical | resources of verse, how perfectly | <u>continued on back flap</u>'; back flap: '<u>continued from front flap</u> | they balance devotion to fact and | to memory and desire, how beauti-|fully they combine toughness and | elegance of mind." | [¶] Since that time Elizabeth | Bishop's reputation has grown | steadily, so that publication of | her collected poems is an even | greater literary event than publi-|cation of <u>North & South</u>. In a | perceptive comment on the present | volume Robert Lowell writes, "Miss | Bishop has a good heart and a | good eye. She has three virtues, | each in itself enough to make a | poet. 1) She knows her own tongue. | Her tone can be Venetian gorgeous | or Quaker simple; she never falls | into cant or miserliness. 2) Her | abundance of description reminds | one, not of poets, poor symbolic, | abstract creatures—but of the | Russian novelists. 3) In all | matters of form: meter, rhythm, | diction, timing, shaping, etc., | she is a master." | [¶] Elizabeth Bishop likes to travel | very much; at present she is | living in Brazil. But the uncom-|promising rocks and the cold sea | air of her native New England | still show in her work. | [¶] " 'The Fish' and 'Roosters' are | two of the most calmly beautiful, | deeply sympathetic poems of our | time. . . . In her best work | restraint, calm, and proportion are | implicit in every detail of metre | or organization or workmanship. | . . . Her work is unusually per-|sonal and honest in its wit, | perception and sensitivity—and | in its restrictions, too; all her | poems have written underneath, | '<u>I have seen it</u>.' " || <u>Randall Jarrell</u>, <u>Poetry and the Age</u> | <u>Knopf, 1953</u> || Jacket by Loren MacIver'.

Text Contents: North & South, reprinted from the 1946 edition;* *A Cold Spring:* "A Cold Spring (for Jane Dewey)," "Over 2000 Illustrations and a Complete Concordance," "The Bight," "A Summer's Dream," "Cape Breton," "At the Fishhouses," "View of the Capital from the Library of Congress," "Insomnia," "The Prodigal," "Faustina, or Rock

**Note:* "The Gentleman of Shalot," was mistitled "The Gentlemen of Shalot" in all printings.

Roses," "Varick Street," "Four Poems: I / Conversation, II / Rain towards Morning, III / While Someone Telephones, IV / O Breath," "Argument," "Letter to N.Y.," "The Mountain," "Invitation to Miss Marianne Moore," "Arrival at Santos," "The Shampoo."

Publication: first printing: 2,000 copies published on July 14, 1955; second printing: 750 copies, 1956; third printing: 500 copies, 1965 (in paper).

Locations: CWM, DLC (deposit copy stamped 5 July 1955, two copies), EB, MoSW (with dust jacket, 2 copies), TxR.

EB to HM (PB), January 2, 1953: As you may remember I wrote once, a long time ago now, that Loren MacIver was interested in doing a jacket for me. I don't know whether she still would be or not, but I think she would—and would undoubtedly do something nice. Would that be a possibility? [¶] I am thinking hard about another title, and I shall try to get the other two poems off to you before the end of the month.

EB to HM (PB), July 28, 1953: I wrote to you some time ago now, five or six months, I think, to ask you about the possibility of publishing "A Cold Spring" sometime soon. . . . [¶] Also I *know* there is a possibility of an English edition, about which I think I've asked you before. English friends keep writing me about when one is to appear and I noticed a while ago I was on the London Times Literary Supplement list for recommended reading in American Poetry. From what I have heard from the English poets I know I feel sure there is an opportunity for this—or possibly some sort of combined edition?

EB to HM (Miss Minahan), September 8, 1953: Here is the copy of *A Cold Spring*—I was sure I sent it about eighteen months ago, before it was published in the New Yorker a year ago last spring. . . . My idea was that it would make a good title poem for a book to be published in the spring.

EB to HM (PB), September 10, 1953: I *measured* the poems & I thought they would come out just about as long as "N & S"—but I may have been mistaken. Would you consider spacing the 4 poems of the "Love Poems" on separate pages?

HM (AO) to EB, April 13, 1954: We are all set to go on *A Cold Spring*, but have a new idea which Paul and I have discussed at some length and which we'd like to try out on you. As you know, *North &*

South is currently out of print and the economics of publishing make a reprinting at this time extremely impractical. As you also know, we are rather worried about the shortness of *A Cold Spring* (it hardly runs to more than 32 pages). It has occurred to us that it might be an excellent idea to combine both books into a third, possibly titled *Concordance*. Not only would this give us a bigger and more saleable book and permit us to bring North & South back into print, but it would also combine into one volume a collection of poems which have a certain unity. I understand that your future work will be something of a departure from everything that we have seen so far. [¶] Mrs. Norah Smallwood, one of the partners of the British firm Chatto & Windus, paid us a visit a few weeks ago. As you may know, they have been following your work with interest for some time and there is a possibility that they might want to do the combined volume in the same format as ours.

EB to HM (AO), April 25, 1954: I am also glad to hear about Chatto and Windus. It seems to me that a combined volume—*North & South*, or the best of *North & South*, and *A Cold Spring*—would be an excellent idea for the English edition. It is what I had in mind myself. However—I have turned against the title "*Concordance*" completely, and I am trying to think of something better to cover the two volumes together. I'll send you another title as soon as I can. [¶] However, after three days thought, it seems to me a combined volume would *not* be a good idea for the U.S. appearance of *A Cold Spring*, nice as it would be to get some of *N & S* back into print again. I have no one here to consult and perhaps I am wrong, of course—but it seems to me that it is so difficult for most people to buy poetry, anyway, that no prospective customer who already had *N & S* would bother to buy it over again. Also, I should imagine that in general my "buying public" would be people who are already familiar with *N & S*, and possibly own it—I mean I don't think the audience for poetry changes much—although perhaps it is enlarging—But I really do not know. Would there be any possibility of doing *both*?—first, say, a small edition of *A Cold Spring*, and then a little later an edition of both—even a cheap paper-cover one? Have you considered any publications like that? I make *A Cold Spring* to be about 40-some pages—I've just measured it and found it a little longer, for example, than Howard Moss's recent, "*The Toy Fair*," Scribners. . . . [¶] P.S. I hope that you can keep the same shape and size of page as the *first* printing of *N & S*. And the same type.

HM (AO) to EB, May 14, 1954: I have again discussed the possibility of combining *North & South* with *A Cold Spring* for a new volume with Paul Brooks and our production manager, and we still believe that in the long run it will be the best plan.

EB to HM (AO), October 2, 1954: I wonder if you could please send me the index I O-K'd for the "Cold Spring" part of the book over again? . . . I thought the order was all right but I began to get the idea that one poem was missing. [¶] There are a couple of things I want to ask you about the book. First: Could that black line that appears throughout "North & South" between the title and the poem proper be left out? Couldn't that be done without too much trouble, or without interfering with the plates otherwise? There was some discussion about it at the time that book was printed and now I've decided that it would really make a much better-looking page if it were simply omitted if that is possible. Will you let me know? [¶] . . . I'd very much like to have that same kind of fabric that was used on "North & South," the *first* printing (the dull blue-grey one, not that bright cheaper-looking one they used later on) again, too, although possibly a different color. [¶] . . . I wonder if you have heard any more from Chatto & Windus? Isn't it a good idea to have books appear as close together as possible, Eng. and American?

HM (AO) to EB, October 19, 1954: I am enclosing the table of contents for *A Cold Spring* as you requested. I wonder if the poem that you thought was missing could be "Insomnia," which you had some doubts about including. As far as everyone here is concerned, it is a very effective poem and should be kept in.

A2.a3 *Poems. North & South—A Cold Spring*. Third printing, [1965] (first edition, third impression, paperback, Smyth sewn)

Poems

NORTH & SOUTH—A COLD SPRING

BY ELIZABETH BISHOP

HOUGHTON MIFFLIN COMPANY BOSTON

The Riverside Press Cambridge

Title Page: 8³⁄₁₆ × 5½ in. (208 × 140 mm.).

THIRD PRINTING   R

Copyright,
1940, 1946, 1947, 1948, 1949, 1951, 1952, 1955,
by Elizabeth Bishop
All rights reserved including the right to reproduce
this book or parts thereof in any form
Library of Congress catalogue card number: 55–7003

The Riverside Press
CAMBRIDGE · MASSACHUSETTS
Printed in the U.S.A.

Pagination: [iii-iv] v [vi] vii-viii, [1–2]3–56 [57–60] 61–93 [94–96].

Paper and Binding: leaf and paper wrapper measure 8³⁄₁₆ × 5½ in. (208 × 140 mm.; yWhite (Centroid 92) wove paper; trimmed from earlier plates; all edges trimmed; glazed v. reddish Orange (34) paper wrapper; front wrapper: '[upper left-hand corner in Black (267)] $3.00 | [on upper half, a p. Yellow Green (121) circle, like a compass, with an ornate v.rO needle running through the center pointing approximately 45° to the right, d. greenish Yellow (103) block letters inside and touching on the upper circumference] POEMS | [horizontal in Black] north | & south | a cold spring | [d.gY block letters inside and touching the lower circumference of the circle] Bishop'; spine: in Black, on p.YG, 'POEMS · BISHOP   HMCO'; back wrapper: in Black, 'Elizabeth Bishop's first volume of poetry *North & South,* | winner of the Houghton Mifflin Poetry Fellowship, was | greeted with critical enthusiasm seldom heard. "At last," | wrote Marianne Moore, "we have a prize book that has no | creditable mannerisms. At last we have someone who knows, | who is not didactic." || Reviewing the poems for *The New Yorker,* Louise Bogan | said, "They strike no attitudes and have not an ounce of | superfluous emotional weight, and they combine an unforced | ironic humor with a naturalist's accuracy of observation, for | Miss Bishop, although she frequently writes fantasy, is | firmly in

$3.00

north
& south
a cold spring

elizabeth

POEMS BISHOP

A2.a3

touch with the real world and takes a Thoreaulike | interest in whatever catches her attention." || When *North and South* was combined with a second collec-|tion, *A Cold Spring*, and published under the title *Poems*, | Elizabeth Bishop received the 1955 Pulitzer Prize for Poetry. | Of this volume Robert Lowell wrote: "Miss Bishop has | a good heart and a good eye . . . She has three virtues, each | in itself enough to make a poet. (1) She knows her own | tongue. Her tone can be Venetian gorgeous or Quaker simple; | she never falls into cant or miserliness. (2) Her abundance | of description reminds one, not of poets, poor symbolic, | abstract creatures—but of the Russian novelists. (3) In all | matters of form: meter, rhythm, diction, timing shaping, | etc., she is a master." || Miss Bishop's long list of honors also includes the Shelley| Memorial Award, The American Academy of Arts and Letters| Award, a Guggenheim Fellowship and the 1964 Fellowship | of the American Academy of Poets.'

Text Contents: same as **A2** except that "The Mountain" has been omitted.

Publication: 500 copies in 1965, at $3.00.

A3 *Poems.* Chatto and Windus, London, 1956 (first edition, first impression)

POEMS

=

Elizabeth Bishop

1956
CHATTO & WINDUS
LONDON

Title Page: 7¾ × 5 in. (196 × 128 mm.).

PUBLISHED BY
CHATTO AND WINDUS LTD
42 WILLIAM IV STREET
LONDON WC2

★

CLARKE, IRWIN AND CO LTD
TORONTO

PRINTED IN ENGLAND
AT THE BLACKMORE PRESS, GILLINGHAM, DORSET
BY T. H. BRICKELL AND SON LTD
ALL RIGHTS RESERVED

Collation: [unsigned 1–2⁸ 3⁴]; 20 leaves; [1–6] 7–40.

Contents: p. 1: half title: 'POEMS'; p. 2: blank; p. 3: title page; p. 4: copyright page; p. 5: 'Contents'; p. 6: 'NOTE | The poems in this book are selected from | *North & South* and *A Cold Spring*'; pp. 7–40: text.

Typography: type page measures 234 ×95 mm., 36 lines per page.

Paper and Binding: leaf measures 7¾ × 5 in. (196 ×128 mm.); yWhite (Centroid 92) laid paper; all edges trimmed; yWhite wove endpapers; l. greenish Yellow (101) laid paper over boards; cover measures 7⅞ × 5³⁄₁₆ in. (200 × 130 mm.); front cover: '[in v.d. bluish Green (166)] POEMS | BY | *Elizabeth Bishop* | [above and beneath these three lines, two reversed vines, each looped in the middle to form a V, with leaves and berries, some solid v.d.bG, some open] | [at bottom, in v.d.bG] CHATTO & WINDUS'; spine and back: blank.

Dust Jacket: same paper and cover design as the boards; printed the same on front; spine: blank; back: 'Poetry | [double rule] | [31 lines of v.d.bG type] | [double rule] | CHATTO & WINDUS | 42 WIL-

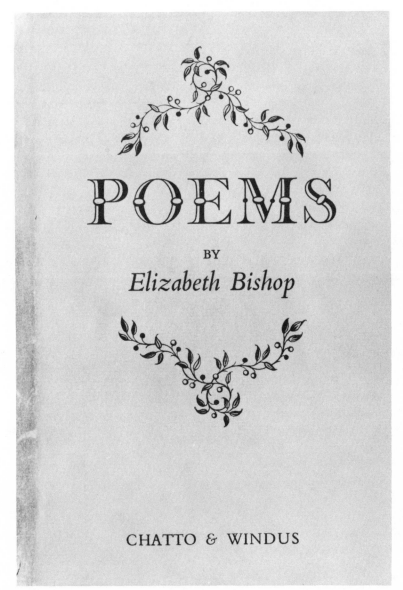

POEMS

BY

Elizabeth Bishop

CHATTO & WINDUS

A3

LIAM IV STREET, LONDON, WC2'; front flap: 'Here is a selection from the work of one of | America's most interesting poets. Miss Bishop is | strongly individual without being eccentric, | humorous but not whimsical. She sees, feels and | thinks for herself: she writes with the assurance of | a sound technique and the authority of first-hand

| experience: her poems are unhampered by | literary fashion, un-clouded by any facile con-|temporary glumness. | [¶] Miss Bishop was awarded the Pulitzer Prize for | Poetry, 1956. || SOME APPRE-CIATIONS OF THE POETRY OF | ELIZABETH BISHOP|| "Elizabeth Bishop seems to me the best American poet | since Emily Dickinson, a truly original talent". | *Walter Allen, The New Statesman* || "She gives the reader a rich world of slow, curious, | strong discoveries, uniquely seen and set. . . . One of | the merits of her poetry is that it is not frustratingly | ambiguous. It is also not highly mysterious". | *Richard Eberhart, New York Times* || "Personal, possessed of wit and sensibility, technically | expert and often moving . . . . In the sum of Miss | Bishop's poetry to the present there is a small group | of poems which can be expected to become a | permanent part of the poetry of our time". | *New York Sunday Herald Tribune* || "Elizabeth Bishop's is a major voice, akin to Wallace | Stevens and Marianne Moore, but speaking for | herself in unmistakable and insistent terms". | *Chicago Sun Times* | [at bottom right] *8s 6d* | *net'*; back flap: an advertisement for The Poetry Book Society.

Text Contents: "The Map," "The Colder the Air," "The Imaginary Iceberg," "Wading at Wellfleet," "The Man-Moth," "Large Bad Picture," "The Unbeliever," "The Weed," "Cirque d'Hiver," "Sleeping Standing Up," "Roosters," "The Fish," "Little Exercise," "Letter to New York," "A Cold Spring," "At the Fishhouses," "The Bight," "Faustina," "The Prodigal," "Invitation to Miss Marianne Moore."

Publication: first printing: 500 copies published on November 14, 1956, at 8/6.

Locations: BL (deposit copy stamped 8 November 1956), CWM, DLC, EB, MoSW (with dust jacket), TxU.

A4 *The Diary of "Helena Morley"*, by Alice (Dayrell) Brant, Farrar, Straus and Cudahy, New York, 1957 (first edition, first impression)

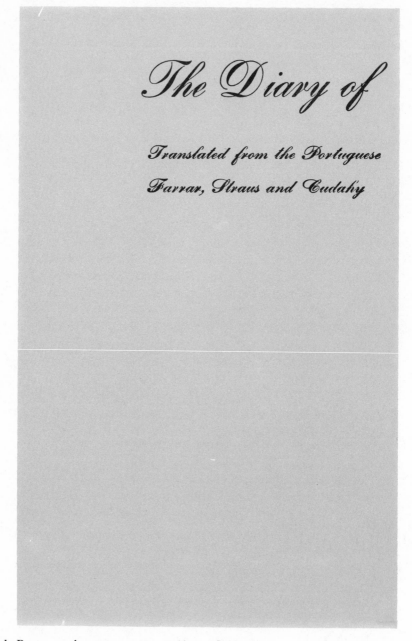

Title Pages: each page measures 8¼ × 5⁷⁄₁₆ in. (209 × 138 mm.)

"Helena Morley"

by Elizabeth Bishop

New York

Collation: [unsigned 1–10^{16}]; 160 leaves; [i–vii] viii–xxxiii [xxxiv–xxxv] xxxvi–xxxvii [xxxviii], [1–3] 4–92 [93] 94–181 [182] 183–281 [282].

Contents: p. i: half title: 'THE DIARY OF "HELENA MORLEY" '; pp. ii–iii: title pages; p. iv: copyright page; p. v: contents; p. vi: blank; pp. vii–xxxiii: 'Introduction'; p. xxxiv: blank; pp. xxxv–xxxvi: 'Author's Preface'; p. xxxvii: 'Letter from George Bernanos to the Author'; p. xxxviii: blank; p. 1: half title; p. 2: blank; pp. 3–281: text; p. 282: blank.

Typography: text: 10/13 Electra × 24 picas; display: Bank script; type page measures 160 × 102 mm.; 36 lines per page including running titles.

Running Titles: pp. viii–xxxiii, upper left-hand corner, opposite the page designation, '*Introduction*'; p. xxxvi, '*Author's Preface*'; pp. 6[even pages]–180, 184–280, '*The Diary of "Helena Morley"*'; pp. 5[odd pages]–91, '*1893*'; pp. 95[odd pages]–181, '*1894*'; pp. 183[odd pages]–281, '*1895*'.

Paper and Binding: leaf measures 8¼ × 5⁷⁄₁₆ in. (209 × 138 mm.); yWhite (Centroid 92) wove paper, possibly from a standard sheet 35 × 22.5 in.; all edges trimmed; upper edges stained v. Yellow (82); front pastedown and endpaper: four black-and-white photographs, identified on pastedown, at lower left: '*a. Outlying district of Diamantina | b. Rua Direita, "Straight Street," the principal street of Diamantina | c. Small church typical of the countryside around Diamantina | d. Corridor in Helena Morley's old school*'; back pastedown and endpaper: black-and-white photograph, identified on endpaper, at lower left: '*Religious procession along Rua Direita. | It was in such processions that Helena |*

THE
DIARY
OF
"HELENA
MORLEY"

Edited by
ELIZABETH
BISHOP

THE
DIARY
OF
"HELENA
MORLEY"

A GIRLHOOD JOURNAL OF LIFE
IN A MOUNTAIN TOWN OF BRAZIL
AT THE TURN OF
THE CENTURY

FARRAR,
STRAUS
AND
CUDAHY

Translated and Edited by
ELIZABETH BISHOP

A4

Morley walked carrying her grandmother's | *gifts of beeswax to be used for candles.*'; d. greenish Gray (156) board cover with a l. greenish Gray (154) geometric pattern of intersecting corners measures 8½ × 5¾ in. (216 × 147 mm.); brill. Yellow (98) cloth spine: '*The Diary of "Helena Morley"* | *Farrar, Straus and Cudahy*'.

Dust Jacket, by Harry Ford: Black (267); front: '[inside border of stylized leaves, s. greenish Blue (169), brill. greenish Yellow (98), deep Yellow Green (118), on Black, centered in White (263)] THE | DIARY | OF | "HELENA | MORLEY" | [in brill.gY] A GIRLHOOD JOURNAL OF LIFE | IN A MOUNTAIN TOWN

a. Outlying district of Diamantina
b. Rua Direita, "Straight Street," the principal street of Diamantina
c. Small church typical of the countryside around Diamantina
d. Corridor in Helena Morley's old school

OF BRAZIL | AT THE TURN OF | THE CENTURY | [outside border in deep YG] *Translated and Edited by* | [in brill.gY] *ELIZABETH BISHOP*'; spine: '[two s.gB leaves] | [in White] 'THE | DIARY | OF | "HELENA | MORLEY" | [in brill.gY] *Edited by* | *ELIZABETH* | *BISHOP* | FARRAR, | STRAUS | AND

A4 (front pastedown endpaper)

| CUDAHY | [two s.gB leaves]'; back: on brill.gY background sur-
rounded by similar s.gB and deep YG leaf design, in Black, '*LETTER
FROM* | *GEORGES BERNANOS* | *TO "HELENA MORLEY"* |
[23 lines of type]'; front flap: on brill.gY, in Black, '$4.75 | THE |
DIARY OF "HELENA MORLEY" | TRANSLATED AND

*Religious procession along Rua Direita.
It was in such processions that Helena
Morley walked carrying her grandmother's
gifts of beeswax to be used for candles.*

A4 (back pastedown endpaper)

EDITED BY | ELIZABETH BISHOP || When Elizabeth Bishop first came to Bra-|zil in 1952 and asked friends which Brazil-|ian books she should begin reading, this | diary was most frequently mentioned. It | had first been published privately in a | small edition in 1942. George Bernanos, | who was living in Brazil in exile, discovered | it [see his statement on back of jacket] and | gave away many copies. Its reputation be-|gan to spread in literary circles, new edi-|tions followed, and now it is a classic. || This is a true diary, kept by a girl between | the ages of twelve and fifteen, in a provin-|cial diamond-mining town called Diaman-|tina, the highest town in Brazil, during the | years 1893 to 1895. Everything in *The | Diary of "Helena Morley"* really did hap-|pen. There really was a Dona Teadora, the | grandmother who managed her family with | an iron will; there really was a Sia Ritinha | who stole her neighbors' but not her em-||(*Continued on back flap*)'; back flap: '(*Continued from front flap*)||ployer's chickens; there really were a Father | Neves, and a spinster English Aunt Madge, | bravely keeping up her standards in a finan-|cially ruined town. || As the translator states, "Much of it | could have happened in any small provin-|cial town or village, and at almost any | period of history—at least before the arrival | of the automobile and the moving-picture | theatre. Certain pages reminded me of | more famous and 'literary' ones: Nausicaa | doing her laundry on the beach, possibly | with the help of *her* freed slaves; bits from | Chaucer; Wordsworth's poetical children | and country people. . ." Miss Bishop | describes one aspect of the Diary as "notes | for an unwritten, Brazilian, feminine ver-|sion of Tom Sawyer and Nigger Jim." | Though the scenes and events of *The | Diary of "Helena Morley"* happened long | ago, what it says, as with all works of art, | is fresh, sad, funny, and eternally true. || JACKET DESIGN BY HARRY FORD || FARRAR, STRAUS AND CUDAHY | 101 FIFTH AVENUE | NEW YORK CITY 3'.

Note: the above is the first state of the jacket. In the second state, the last line of the front flap and the first line of the back flap read: 'who stole her neighbors' but not the Mor-|ley chickens; there really were a Father . . .'.

Text Contents: "Introduction," "1893," "1894," and "1895."

Publication: first printing: 4,000 copies published on December 16, 1957, at $4.75; second printing: 2,000 copies, 1958.

Note: EB first proposed this project to Houghton Mifflin. Her letters to Houghton Mifflin dated July 28, 1953, August 2, 1954, Sunday—August ?—1954, September 7, 1954, and October 2, 1954, mention this project (Houghton Library, bMs Am 1925 [205]).

Locations: CWM, DLC, EB, MoSW (with dust jacket), TxR.

A4.[b1]* *The Diary of "Helena Morley"*, by Alice (Dayrell) Brant. The Ecco Press, New York, [1977] (paperback proof copy)

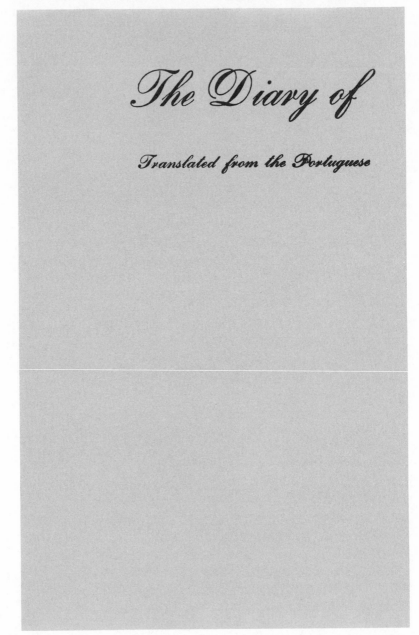

Title Pages: each page measures 8¼ × 5⁷⁄₁₆ in. (211 × 138 mm.).

"Helena Morley"

by Elizabeth Bishop

Elizabeth Bishop — N.Y. nov. 30th
1977
(minus the foreword added in June 1977)

ECCO PRESS

New York

The Diary of

"Helena Morley"

Translated from the Portuguese

by Elizabeth Bishop

Galley no.:_____ Pub. date: 11/77 Price: 4.95

Unrevised proofs. Confidential. Please do not quote for publication until verified with finished book.

The Ecco Press

A4.[b1]* (proof cover)

Imprint: none.

Collation: [unsigned 1₁ 2–11¹⁶ 12₁]; 162 leaves; [1–2], [i–vii] viii–xxxiii [xxxiv–xxxv] xxxvi–xxxvii [xxxviii], [1–3] 4–92 [93] 94–181 [182] 183–281 [282–284].

Contents: same as A4, except for the first and last leaves, both blank. On the recto of the first leaf, hand stamped in black, is: 'Antaeus | The Ecco Press | 1 West 30th Street | New York, N.Y. 10001'.

Typography: same as A4, except for the type used for the publisher.

Running Titles: same as A4.

Paper and Binding: leaf and paper wrapper measure 8¼ × 5⁷⁄₁₆ in (211 × 138 mm.); yWhite (Centroid 92) wove paper; all edges trimmed; unglazed l. bluish Green (163) paper wrapper; front wrapper: '*The Diary of* | *"Helena Morley"* | *Translated from the Portuguese* | *by Elizabeth Bishop* | [figures handwritten] Galley No. ___ Pub. date 11/77 Price: 4.95 | Unrevised proofs. Confidential. Please do not quote | for publication until verified with finished book. | The Ecco Press'; spine and back: blank.

Text Contents: same as A4.

Location: CWM.

A4.[b1] *The Diary of "Helena Morley"*, by Alice (Dayrell) Brant, The Ecco Press, New York, [1977] (first edition, fifth impression from offset plates from the first edition, paperback, Smyth sewn)

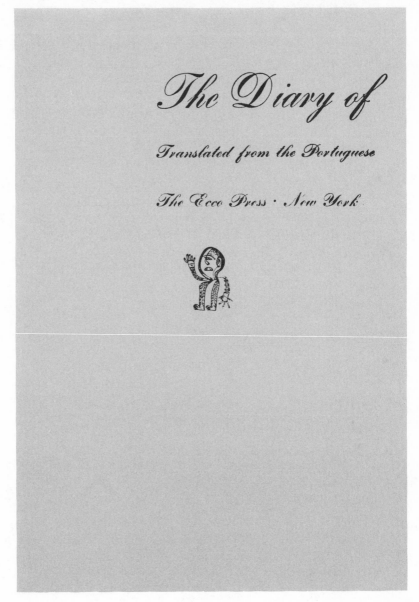

Title Pages: each page measures 8¼ × 5⁷⁄₁₆ in. (211 × 138 mm.).

"Helena Morley"

by Elizabeth Bishop

Library of Congress Cataloging in Publication Data
Brant, Alice Dayrell.
   The diary of "Helena Morley."
   Translation of Minha vida de menina.
   1.   Brant, Alice Dayrell.
   2.   Diamantina, Brazil—Biography.
F2651.D5B7213   1977   981'.5   [B]   77-2327
ISBN 0-912-94646-6

This edition published by arrangement with
Farrar, Straus & Giroux, Inc.
Cover design by Cynthia Krupat.

Collation: [unsigned 1–10^{16}]; 160 leaves; [i–vii] viii [ix] x–xxxv [xxxvi] xxxvii [xxxviii], [1–3] 4–92 [93] 94–181 [182] 183–281 [282–284].

Contents: p. i: half title; pp. ii–iii: title pages; p. iv: copyright page; p. v: contents; p. vi: blank; pp. vii–viii: 'Foreword'; pp. ix–xxxv: 'Introduction'; pp. xxxvi–xxxvii: 'Author's Preface'; p. xxxviii: 'Letter from Georges Bernanos to the Author'; p. 1: half title; p. 2: blank; pp. 3–281: text; p. 282: blank.

Typography: same as A4.

Paper and Binding: leaf and paper wrapper measure 8¼ × 5⁷⁄₁₆ in. (211 × 138 mm.); yWhite (Centroid 92) wove paper; White (263), Black (267), d. Blue (183), v. greenish Yellow (97), and deep greenish

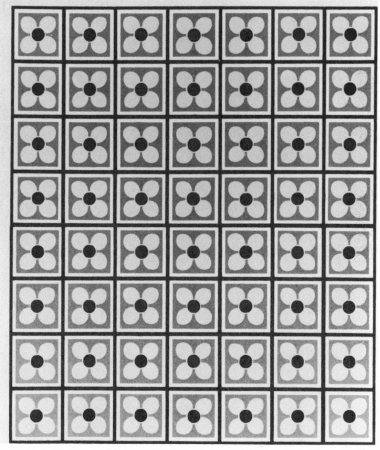

THE DIARY OF
"Helena Morley"
Translated and edited by E L I Z A B E T H   B I S H O P

A4.[b1]

Yellow (100) glazed paper wrapper; front wrapper: in Black, 'THE
DIARY OF | *"HELENA MORLEY"* | [rule] | *Translated and
edited by* ELIZABETH BISHOP' | [a geometric pattern of 56 v.gY
flowers with d.B centers on deep gY edged in White within 56 d.B

squares beneath title] | spine: vertical, in Black, 'THE DIARY OF "*HELENA MORLEY*" | [rule] | ELIZABETH BISHOP ECCO'; back wrapper: '[in d. Blue] $4.95 | [in Black] THE DIARY OF "*HELENA MORLEY*" | TRANSLATED AND EDITED BY ELIZABETH BISHOP | *Neglected Books of the Twentieth Century* | [rule] || *This is a true diary, kept by a young Brazilian girl in a provin-| cial | diamond-mining town called Diamantina, at the end of the nine-| teenth century. First published privately in Brazil in 1942, the | diary gained a reputation in literary circles, and is now considered | a classic. Though the scenes and events happened long ago, what | this book says is fresh, sad, funny, and eternally true.* || "Let no one say that books are no longer interesting. I feel that | this *Diary of "Helena Morley"* has poetry, narrative, and philosophy. How fortunate Dona Alice is to have her words so rarely | (sensitively) translated." —*Marianne Moore* || "It reminds us that being young is a wonderful thing, that aware-|ness is not inconsistent with high spirits, and that the gifted child | is not necessarily the tortured one." —*The Atlantic Monthly* || "It gives an extraordinarily detailed and vivid picture of a small-|town world seen with the fresh, sharp eye of an exuberant young-|ster who had great zest for life in all of its phases." | —*Saturday Review* | [rule] || *The Ecco Press, 1 West 30th Street, New York 10001* | *Distrib-uted by The Viking Press, 625 Madison Avenue, New York 10022* | [device] | [in bottom right corner, in d.B] SBN: 912–94646–6'.

Text Contents: the same as **A4** with some corrections and an additional "Foreword," by EB.

Publication: first printing: 3,158 copies published in December 1977, at $4.95.

Note: The following lines were reset:

viii/x.29   child-likeness] childlikeness
xiv/xvi.25   [reset with xiv/xvi.26]
xiv/xvi.26   deceptively] looking ~
xxii/xxiv.29
xxv/xxvii.16   word] product
3.fn.   xxxiii] xxxv
9.2   were] was
10.fn.2   Script] Scrib
10.fn.6   script] scrib

10.fn.7   [reset with 10.fn.6]
11.2 dining room] dining-room
16.fn.   *Cachaça*] Cachaça
19.fn.
23.32   grownups] grown-ups
24.8   ant's] ants'
24.9   ant's] ants'
28.15
28.25   water-falls] waterfalls
30.18 can] can't
32.6   theater] theatre
36.8   Julia] Júlia
39.26
43.32
45.3   peanut-brittle] peanut brittle
50.26   peanut-brittle] peanut brittle
54.4   criticise] criticize
54.31
55.3
58.24   criticise] criticize
63.22   god-daughter] goddaughter
79.10   babtise] baptize
91.24   Mama] mama
94.23   Heaven] heaven
96.fn.1   [reset to match 96.fn.3]
96.fn.3   *Calderão;*] Calderão:
97.13   living room] living-room
97.14   [reset with 97.13 and 97.15]
97.15   living room] living-room
102.13   School] school
113.12   bad mannered] bad-mannered
119.19   diamond cutting] diamond-cutting
123.9   vegatable] vegetable
129.28   father,] ~.
133.3   S.] St.
137.11   mass] Mass
141.15   dumb bells] dumbbells
151.22   Julia] Júlia
151.fn.2   at present servants] in the country ~
151.fn.3   [reset with 151.fn.2]

157.fn.   xviii] xix
162.fn.3   god-parent] godparent
162.fn. 4   co-god-parent] co-godparent
167.9   to] too
169.8   mass] Mass
185.17   mass] Mass
185.19   mass] Mass
186.3   country,] ~ˌ
186.4   [reset with 186.3]
186.17   Mama] mama
197.29   marvelous] marvellous
198.11   god-sent] godsend
200.8   So-and-So] So-and-so
223.19   babtise] baptize
226.fn.2   *Nursing.*] ~ˌ
226.fn.3   Nightingale]ˌ] Nightingale].
231.22   'I've] "~
233.5   School] school
233.14   School] school
233.31   School] school
236.22   school-teacher] schoolteacher
258.2   finihed] finished
258.11   People'] ~"
262.21   mass] Mass
263.5   *milreis*] *mil reis*
263.25–26   [reset due to broken type]
272.8   Luizinhaˌ] Luizinha,
275.29   barrased] barrassed
277.12   dining room] dining-room
278   [running head reset due to broken type]

A4.[c1]   *The Diary of "Helena Morley"*, by Alice (Dayrell) Brant, Victor Gollancz, London, 1958 (first edition, third impression, produced by offset or from the plates of the first impression)

The Diary of

"Helena Morley"

Translated from the Portuguese

by Elizabeth Bishop

LONDON
VICTOR GOLLANCZ LTD
1958

Title Page: 7¹¹/₁₆ × 5 in. (202 × 132 mm.).

PRINTED IN GREAT BRITAIN BY
LOWE AND BRYDONE (PRINTERS) LIMITED, LONDON, N.W.10

Collation: signed [A^{16}] B–I^{16} K^{16}; 160 leaves; [i–vii] viii–xxxiii [xxxiv–xxxv] xxxvi–xxxvii [xxxviii], [1–3] 4–92 [93] 94–181 [182] 183–281 [282].

Contents: p. i: half title: 'THE DIARY OF "HELENA MORLEY" '; p. ii: blank; p. iii: title page; p. iv: copyright page; p. v: contents; p. vi: blank; pp. vii–xxxiii: 'Introduction'; p. xxxiv: blank; pp. xxxv–xxxvi: 'Author's Preface'; p. xxxvii: 'Letter from Georges Bernanos to the Author'; p. xxxviii: blank; p. 1: half title; p. 2: blank; pp. 3–281: text; p. 282: blank.

Typography: same as **A4**.

Running Titles: same as **A4**.

Paper and Binding: leaf measures 7^{11}⁄₁₆ × 5 in. (196 × 128 mm.); yWhite (Centroid 92.5) wove paper; all edges trimmed; yWhite wove endpapers; unglazed d. Red (16) cloth cover measures 7^{15}⁄₁₆ × 5^{3}⁄₁₆ in. (202 × 132 mm); spine: in gold, 'THE | DIARY | OF | "HE-LENA | MORLEY" | GOLLANCZ'.

Dust Jacket: front: '[in White (263) on Black (267)] THE DIARY OF | 'HELENA MORLEY' | [deep Blue (179) stripe] | [in Black on s. Yellow (84)] *Letter from Bernanos to 'Helena Morley'* | [17 lines of type] | [deep B stripe] | [in White on Black] Translated by | ELIZABETH BISHOP'; spine: in Black on s.Y, 'The | DIARY OF | HELENA | MORLEY | by | ELIZABETH | BISHOP | [publisher's device] | GOLLANCZ'; back: White, blank; front flap: '*The Diary of* | *'Helena Morley'* | [¶] When Elizabeth Bishop first |

THE DIARY OF 'HELENA MORLEY'

Letter from Bernanos to 'Helena Morley'

YOU HAVE WRITTEN one of those books, so rare in any literature, that owe nothing to either experience or talent, but everything to *ingenium*, to genius—for we should not be afraid of that much misused word— to genius drawn from its very source, to the genius of adolescence. Because these recollections of a simple little girl of Minas present the same problem as the dazzling poems of Rimbaud. As vastly different as they may appear to the stupid, we know that they are both of them derived from the same mysterious and magical fountain—of life and of art.

It is possible that you do not even know the value of what you have given us. As for me, who feel it so deeply, I would not know how to define it.

You have made us see and love everything that you saw and loved yourself in those days, and every time I close your book I am more than ever convinced that its secret will always escape me. But what does that matter? It is deeply moving to realize that the little girl that you were and the little universe in which she lived will never die.

Please accept my homage.   GEORGES BERNANOS

Translated by

ELIZABETH BISHOP

GOLLANCZ

A4.[c1]

went to Brazil in 1952 and asked | friends which Brazilian books she | should begin reading, this diary | was most frequently mentioned. | It had first been published pri-|vately in a small edition in 1942. | Georges Bernanos, who was living | in Brazil in exile, discovered it (see | his letter on the front of this | jacket) and gave away many | copies. Its reputation began to | spread in literary circles, new | editions fol-lowed, and now it is a | classic. | [¶] This is a true diary, kept by a | girl between the ages of twelve and | fifteen, in a provincial dia-mond-|mining town called Diamantina, | the highest town in Brazil, during | the years 1893 and 1895. The | author, who is half-English, is | now seventy-six. | [¶] As the translator says, "Much | of it could have happened in any | small provincial town or village, | and at almost any period of | history—at least before the arrival | of the automobile and the moving-|picture theatre. Certain pages | reminded me of more famous and | [*please turn to back flap* | 18/– | net'; back flap: 'literary ones: Nausicaa doing | her laundry on the beach, possibly | with the help of *her* freed slaves; | bits from Chaucer; Wordsworth's | poetical children and country | people . . ." And Miss Bishop | justly describes one aspect of the | Diary as "notes for an unwritten, | Brazilian, feminine version of Tom | Sawyer and Nigger Jim." | [¶] Here is the voice of nature | speaking to us in the idiom of art: | and what it says is fresh, sad, | funny and eternally true.'

Text Contents: same as **A4**.

Publication: first printing: 1,500 copies published on September 8, 1958, at 18/– net; second printing: 500 copies, June [1959].

Locations: CWM, EB, MoSW (with dust jacket).

Note: this edition and **A4** differ in their title and copyright pages. The running head (p. 278) is not broken, but the type in l. 25–26, p. 263 is the same as that in the first impression. However, the paper of this edition is thinner and the binding is considerably cheaper.

A5 *Brazil.* Time Incorporated, New York, 1962 (first edition, first impression)

LIFE WORLD LIBRARY

BRAZIL

by Elizabeth Bishop
and The Editors of LIFE

TIME INCORPORATED   NEW YORK

Title Page: 10¾ × 8⅜ in. (273 × 212 mm.) 'BRAZIL' printed in d. bluish Green (Centroid 165).

Colophon: p. 160: '*Production staff for Time Incorporated | Arthur R. Murphy (Vice President and Director of Production) | Robert E. Foy, James P. Menton and Caroline Ferri | Text photocomposed on Photon*

COVER: Misty clouds drift
across the rounded *morros*,
the hills which keep
Rio de Janeiro huddled close
by the Atlantic Ocean.

ABOUT THE WRITER

Elizabeth Bishop, the author of the interpretive text for this volume of
the LIFE World Library, is an American poet who has made her home in
Brazil since 1952. Widely acquainted in diplomatic, journalistic and artis-
tic circles, she has traveled throughout the country, voyaging to the deso-
late Mato Grosso jungles and far up the Amazon. Born and brought up
in New England, Miss Bishop graduated from Vassar and has been publishing verse and prose for more than 25 years. Her two volumes of
poetry, *North & South* and *A Cold Spring*, in conjunction with work in U.S.
magazines, won her the Pulitzer Prize in 1956.

Brazil © 1962 by Time Inc. All rights reserved. Simultaneously published in Canada.
Library of Congress catalog card number 62-11737.

equipment | *under the direction of Albert J. Dunn and Arthur J. Dunn* |
[device] | *Printed by R. R. Donnelley & Sons Company, Crawfordsville,
Indiana,* | *and The Safran Printing Company, Detroit, Michigan* |
Bound by R. R. Donnelley & Sons Company, Crawfordsville, Indiana |
Paper by The Mead Corporation, Dayton, Ohio'.

Collation: [unsigned 1–10^8]; 80 leaves; pp. [1–7] 8–160.

Contents: p. i: half title: 'LIFE WORLD LIBRARY | BRAZIL'; p. 2:
'OTHER BOOKS BY THE EDITORS OF LIFE | LIFE'S Picture
History of World War II | LIFE'S Picture History of Western Man
| The World We Live In | *with Lincoln Barnett* | The World's Great
Religions | America's Arts and Skills | Picture Cook Book | The
The Second World War | *with Winston S. Churchill* | The Wonders
of Life on Earth | *with Lincoln Barnett* | LIFE Pictorial Atlas of the

A5

World | *with the Editors of Rand McNally* | LIFE Nature Library | The Epic of Man | The LIFE Treasury of American Folklore'; p. 3: title page; p. 4: copyright page; p. 5: 'Contents'; p. 6: editorial page; p. 7: 'Introduction'; pp. 8–151: text; pp. 152–155: 'Appendix'; p. 156: 'Credits'; p. 157–160: 'Index'.

Paper and Binding: leaf measures 10¾ × 8⅜ in. (273 × 212 mm.); White (Centroid 263.5) glossy laid paper; all edges trimmed; front endpapers and pastedown: in gWhite (153), l. greenish Gray (154), v.l. bluish Green (162) and Black (267), 'BRAZIL Political Map'; back pastedown and endpaper: in same colors, 'BRAZIL Relief Map'; glazed cloth cover measures 11 × 8⅝ in. (280 × 218 mm.); front cover: in l. Gray (264), on White (263), '[LIFE trademark] WORLD LIBRARY | BRAZIL' followed by color photograph of Rio de Janiero and the Atlantic Ocean; spine: vertical, 'BRAZIL [LIFE trademark] WORLD LIBRARY'; back cover: deep Brown (56) with White globe, centered.

Dust Jacket: none.

Text Contents: "Introduction," "Chapter 1: A Warm and Reasonable People," "Chapter 2: Undeveloped Land of Legend," "Chapter 3: Century of Honor and Pride," "Chapter 4: Shifting Centers for Government," "Chapter 5: The Slow Awakening Giant," "Chapter 6: Graceful and Popular Skills," "Chapter 7: A Merited Respect for the Arts," "Chapter 8: A Changing Social Scene," "Chapter 9: The Struggle for a Stable Democracy," "Chapter 10: A Nation Perplexed and Uncertain."

Publication: first printing: 250,000 copies available by mail published on February 10, 1962, at $2.95.

Locations: CWM, DLC, EB, MoSW, TxR, TxU.

Note: In Robert Wilson's copy Elizabeth Bishop corrected the title page so that it reads: "some by Elizabeth Bishop; and more by The Editors of LIFE." Miss Bishop, in the George Starbuck interview (Q10), details her relationship with the Editors of *Life*. When the book was revised in 1963, Miss Bishop was asked to rewrite the political chapters, but refused, nor did she do any of the work concerning the four subsequent revisions. There were five foreign editions, including a heavily revised English one (with dust jacket) done by Time-Life International, which is not described here. The book was never translated into Portuguese.

EB to CWM, May 17, 1978: Could you say that ALL of the chapter headings were concocted by LIFE? Not one of my original chapter headings was used.

A6 *Questions of Travel*. Farrar, Straus and Giroux, New York, 1965 (first edition, first impression)

Elizabeth Bishop

QUESTIONS OF TRAVEL

Farrar, Straus and Giroux
New York

Title Page: 8½ × 6⅛ in. (216 × 155 mm.).

Collation: [unsigned 1–7⁸]; 56 leaves; [i–xii], [1–2] 3–44 [45–46] 47–95 [96–100].

Contents: p. i: half title: 'QUESTIONS OF TRAVEL'; p. ii: blank; p. iii: '*Books by Elizabeth Bishop* | NORTH AND SOUTH | A COLD SPRING | POEMS (*combined volume*) | QUESTIONS OF TRAVEL | THE DIARY OF HELENA MORLEY (*translation*)'; p. iv: blank; p. v: title page; p. vi: copyright page; p. vii: dedication: 'For Lota de Macedo Soares | . . . *O dar-vos quanto tenho e quanto posso,* | *Que quanto mais vos pago, mais vos devo.* | Camões'; p. viii: blank; p. ix: acknowledgments; p. x: blank; p. xi: '*Contents*'; p. xii: blank; p. 1: half title: '*BRAZIL*'; p. 2: blank; p. 3–44: text; p. 45: half title: '*ELSEWHERE*'; p. 46: blank; pp. 47–95: text; pp. 96–100: blank.

Typography: text: 12/15 Linotype Granjon; display: Monotype Janson; type page measures 170 × 110 mm., 24 lines of text per page.

Watermark: 'CURTIS RAG'.

Paper and Binding: leaf measures 8½ × 6⅛ in. (216 × 155 mm.); yWhite (Centroid 92) laid paper; top and fore edges trimmed; bottom edges rough trimmed; top edges stained deep Purple (219); m. Olive Green (125) endpapers; s. greenish Blue (169) cloth cover measures 8¾ × 6¼ in. (222 × 158 mm.); spine: vertical, '[in d. Blue (183)] *Elizabeth Bishop* [in silver] QUESTIONS OF TRAVEL [in brill. Yellow Green (116)] *Farrar, Straus and Giroux*'.

Dust Jacket, by Adrianne Onderdonk: front, superimposed on a map of the *Nuevo Mundo* in deep Purple (219) and greenish Blue (173.5), '[in White (263)] *Questions | of Travel* | [in brill. Yellow Green (116)] *poems by Elizabeth | Bishop*'; spine: vertical, '[in White] *Questions of Travel* [in brill.YG] *Elizabeth Bishop* [in White] *Farrar, Straus | and Giroux*'; back, black-and-white drawing of Elizabeth Bishop labeled: '*Drawing by Darcy Penteado | Elizabeth Bishop*'; front flap: '$3.95 | Elizabeth Bishop | Questions | of Travel || The publication of this book is a lit-|erary event. It is Miss Bishop's first | volume of verse since *Poems*, which | was awarded the Pulitzer Prize for | Poetry in 1955. | [¶] This new collection consists of two | parts. Under the general heading "Bra-|zil" are grouped eleven poems includ-|ing "Manuelzinho," "The Armadillo," | "Twelfth Morning, or What You | Will," "The Riverman," "Brazil, Jan-|uary 1, 1502" and the title poem. The | second section, entitled "Elsewhere," | includes among others "First Death in | Nova Scotia," "Manners," "Sand-|piper," "From Trollope's Journal," | and "Visits to St. Elizabeths." In addi-|tion to the poems there is an extraor-|dinary story of a Nova Scotia child-|hood, "In the Village." || (*continued on back flap*)'; back flap: '(*continued from front flap*) | [¶] Robert Lowell has recently written, | "I am sure no living poet is as curious | and observant as Miss Bishop. What | cuts so deep is that each poem is in-|spired by her own tone, a tone of | large, grave tenderness and sorrowing | amusement. She is too sure of herself | for empty mastery and breezy plagi-|arism, too interested for confession | and musical monotony, too powerful | for mismanaged fire, and too civilized | for idiosyncratic incoherence. She has | a humorous, commanding genius for | picking up the unnoticed, now making | something sprightly and right, and | now a great monument. Once her | poems, each shining, were too few. | Now they are many. When we read | her, we enter the classical serenity of | a new country." || Jacket design by ADRIANNE ONDERDONK, after | a map of the *Nuevo Mundo* in the *Cosmo-|graphia* of Sebastian

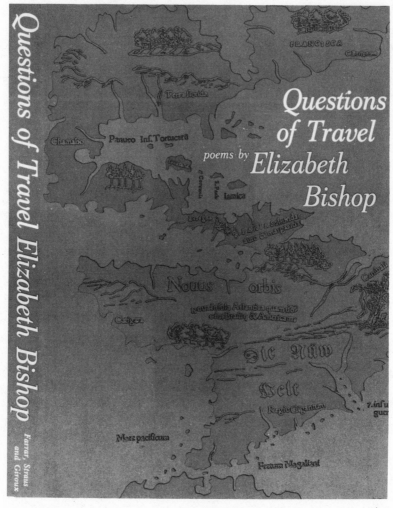

A6

Munster, 16th century | cartographer. (*Archives of the New York | Public Library*) || FARRAR, STRAUS AND GIROUX | 19 Union Square West | New York City 10003'.

Text Contents: "I. Brazil": "Arrival at Santos," reprinted from *Poems: North & South—A Cold Spring*; "Brazil, January 1, 1502"; "Questions of Travel"; "Squatter's Children"; "Manuelzinho"; "Electrical Storm"; "Song for the Rainy Season"; "The Armadillo (for Robert Lowell)"; "The Riverman"; "Twelfth Morning; or What You Will"; "The

Burglar of Babylon"; "II. Elsewhere": "In the Village"; "Manners (for a Child of 1918)"; "Sestina"; "First Death in Nova Scotia"; Filling Station"; "Sunday, 4 A.M."; "Sandpiper"; "From Trollope's Journal"; "Visits to St. Elizabeths."

Publication: first printing: 4,000 copies on November 29, 1965, at $3.95; second printing: 900 copies, 1966 (in cloth); first Noonday printing: 4,000 copies, 1967 (in paper); third printing: 1,300 copies, 1968 (in cloth).

Locations: CWM, DLC (deposit copy stamped 6 December 1965), EB, MoSW (with dust jacket), TxR, TxU.

A6.[b1] *Questions of Travel.* The Noonday Press, New York, 1967
(first edition, third impression, paperback, Smyth sewn)

Elizabeth Bishop

QUESTIONS
OF TRAVEL

The Noonday Press,
a division of Farrar, Straus and Giroux
New York

Title Page: 8³/₁₆ × 5½ in. (210 × 140 mm.).

Collation: [unsigned 1–2^{16} 3^8 4^{16}]; 56 leaves; [i–xii], [1–2] 3–44 [45–46] 47–95 [96–100].

Typography: same as A6.

Paper and Binding: leaf and paper wrapper measure 8³⁄₁₆ × 5½ in. (210 × 140 mm.); yWhite (Centroid 89.5) wove paper (see note); all edges trimmed; glazed m. greenish Blue (173) paper wrapper, front and spine resemble the dust jacket of A6, back is White (263); front wrapper: '[in White] *Questions | of Travel* | [in brill. Yellow Green (116)] *poems by Elizabeth | Bishop* | Noonday 323 | $1.95'; spine: vertical, '[in White] *Questions of Travel* [in brill.YG] *Elizabeth Bishop* [in White] Noonday 323 N323 [publisher's device]'; back wrapper: in m.gB on White, 'N 323 Poetry $1.95 | Elizabeth Bishop | QUESTIONS OF TRAVEL | [¶] This is Elizabeth Bishop's first volume of verse since *Poems*, | which was awarded the Pulitzer Prize for Poetry in 1955. It | consists of two parts, entitled "Brazil" and "Elsewhere," and in | addition to the poems there is the extraordinary story of a Nova | Scotia

A6.b1

childhood, "In the Village." || ROBERT LOWELL: | [¶] "I am sure no living poet is as curious and observant as Miss | Bishop. What cuts so deep is that each poem is inspired by her | own tone, a tone of large, grave tenderness and sorrowing amuse-|ment. . . . When we read her, we enter the classical serenity | of a new country." || GENE BARO, *New York Times Book Review:* | [¶]*"Questions of Travel* shows Eliza-beth Bishop at the full ma-|turity of her powers. . . . This book is a formidable achievement." || HOWARD MOSS, *Kenyon Review:* | [¶] "Admired by critics, poets, and anyone genuinely interested | in writing, Elizabeth Bishop's work is not easily labeled. . . . She | is a poet pure and simple who has perfect pitch. These new | poems should be welcomed not only because they are so abso-|lutely and obviously first-rate but because they are one of the | few examples of lucidity left in the world." || PHILIP BOOTH, *Christian Science Monitor:* | [¶]*"Questions of Travel* asks much of the world it defines, and | pro-vides at least one answer to be grateful for: Miss Bishop is | not only our most valuable export to Brazil, she is one of the | few true poets of this, or any hemisphere." || *Cover design by Adrianne Onderdonk,* | *after a map by Sebastian Munster, 16th century cartographer* || THE NOON-DAY PRESS | 19 Union Square West New York 10003'.

Text Contents: same as **A6**.

Publication: 4,000 copies in 1967, at $1.95.

Locations: CWM, MoSW, ViU.

Note: The paper in this book is of poor quality; consequently, all copies yellowed very quickly.

A7 *Selected Poems*. Chatto and Windus, London, 1967 (first edition, first impression)

SELECTED
POEMS

Elizabeth Bishop

1967

CHATTO & WINDUS

LONDON

Title Page: 5 7/16 × 8½ in. (215 × 138 mm.).

Published by
Chatto and Windus Ltd
42 William IV Street
London WC2

The poems in this volume are selected from
North & South, A Cold Spring, and *Questions of Travel*

© Elizabeth Bishop 1967
Copyright 1940, 1946, 1947, 1948, 1949, 1951, © 1952, 1953,
1955, 1956, 1957, 1958, 1959, 1960, 1961, 1962, 1964. 1965
by Elizabeth Bishop

Printed in Great Britain by
T. H. Brickell and Son Ltd
Gillingham, Dorset

Collation: signed A-G⁸ H²; 58½ leaves; [1–8] 9–39 [40–42] 43–64 [65–66]67–102 [103–104] 105–117 [117 printed on back flyleaf].

Contents: p. 1: half title: 'SELECTED POEMS'; p. 2: '*By the same author* | [device] | POEMS | (1956) | THE DIARY OF HELENA MORLEY | (Translation) | (*Published by Victor Gollancz Ltd.*)'; p. 3: title page; p. 4: copyright page; pp. 5–6: '*Contents*'; p. 7: half title: '*From* NORTH & SOUTH'; p. 8: blank; pp. 9–39: text; p. 40: blank; p. 41: half title: '*From* A COLD SPRING'; p. 42: dedication: 'To Dr. Anny Baumann'; pp. 43–64: text; p. 65: half title: '*From* QUESTIONS OF TRAVEL | I Brazil'; p. 66: dedication: 'For Lota de Macedo Soares | . . . *O dar-vos quanto tenho e quanto posso,* | *Que quanto mais pago, mais vos devo.* | Camões'; pp. 67–102: text; p. 103: half title: '*From* QUESTIONS OF TRAVEL | II Elsewhere'; p. 104: blank; pp. 105–117: text.

Paper and Binding: leaf measures 5⁷⁄₁₆ × 8½ in. (215 × 138 mm.); yWhite (Centroid 92) wove paper; all edges trimmed; yWhite wove endpapers; unglazed brill. Blue (177.5) cloth cover measures 8¹³⁄₁₆ × 5⅝ in. (221 × 142 mm.); spine: in gold, '[vertical] SELECTED POEMS ~ Elizabeth Bishop | [horizontal] C | W'.

Dust Jacket: in White (263.5) with m. Blue (182) and v. Red (11) threads; front: all inside a double s. Blue (178.5) rule with a design between, '[in Black (267)] ELIZABETH | BISHOP | [s.B device] | [in Black] *Selected Poems*'; spine: vertical, '[in Black] *Selected Poems*—[in s.B] *Elizabeth Bishop* [in Black] *Chatto & Windus*'; back: '[in s.B] Poetry by Americans | [20 lines in Black] | [in s.B] CHATTO & WINDUS, LONDON'; front flap: 'For this new volume, her first to be | published in England in more than a | decade, the distinguished American poet | Elizabeth Bishop has selected forty-four | poems from all of her published books. The | selection includes such famous pieces as | 'Roosters', 'At the Fishhouses' and 'The | Man-Moth' from her early volumes *North | & South* and *A Cold Spring*; eleven poems | with Brazilian settings from her recent | volume *Questions of Travel*; and, from the | same book, a group headed 'Elsewhere | which ends with her poem on Ezra Pound, | 'Visits to St. Elizabeths'. | [¶] Miss Bishop was awarded the Pulitzer | Prize for Poetry for her 1955 volume | *Poems*, and she has received many other | honours and awards. Her contemporary | Robert Lowell has written in praise of her | work: 'I am sure no living poet is as | curious and observant as Miss Bishop.... | She has a humorous, commanding genius | for picking up the unnoticed, now making | something sprightly and right, and now a | great monument. Once her poems, each | shining, were too few. Now they are many. | When we read her, we enter the classical | serenity of a new country. || [lower right] 21s. | net'; back flap: 'ELIZABETH BISHOP was born in | New England and spent her childhood in | Nova Scotia. She has lived in Florida and | in Maine, as well as in New York City, has | travelled very widely abroad, and now | makes her home in Brazil. In addition to | her poetry, she has published a translation | from the Portuguese of the Brazilian | classic, *The Diary of Helena Morley*. || Chatto & Windus Ltd. | 42 William IV Street | London W.C.2 || *Mackays of Chatham*'.

Text Contents: from *North & South*: "The Map," "The Imaginary Iceberg," "The Colder the Air," "From the Country to the City," "The Man-Moth," "A Miracle for Breakfast," "Large Bad Picture," "The Monument," "Cirque d'Hiver," "Florida," "Jerónimo's House," "The Fish," "Cootchie," "Songs for a Colored Singer," "Roosters";

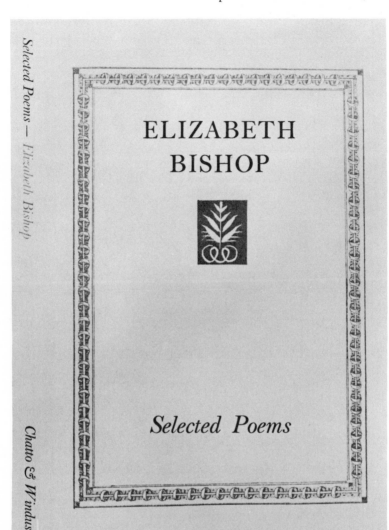

A7

from *A Cold Spring*: "Over 2000 Illustrations and a Complete Concordance," "The Bight," "Faustina, or Rock Roses," "A Summer's
Dream," "Cape Breton," "At the Fishhouses," "The Prodigal," "Varick Street," "Two Poems (Rain towards Morning; While Someone
Telephones)," "Invitation to Miss Marianne Moore," "The Shampoo";
from *Questions of Travel*: "Arrival at Santos," "Brazil, January 1,
1502," "Questions of Travel," "Squatter's Children," "Manuelzinho,"

"Electrical Storm," "Song for the Rainy Season," "The Armadillo," "The Riverman," "Twelfth Morning; or What You W ll," "The Burglar of Babylon," "Manners," "Sestina," "First Dea h in Nova Scotia," "Filling Station," "Sandpiper," "From Trollope's Journal," "Visits to St. Elizabeths."

Publication: first printing: 1,200 copies published on October 26, 1967, at 21/– net.

Locations: BL (deposit copy stamped 6 October 1967), CWM, DEU, DLC (stamped 6 November 1967), EB, MoSW (with dust jacket).

A8 *The Ballad of the Burglar of Babylon.* Farrar, Straus and Giroux, New York, 1968 (first edition, first impression)

Title Pages: each page measures 9¼ × 7¾ in. (234 × 196 mm.). Woodcut of two d. Yellow (Centroid 85) buzzards flying in the m. greenish Blue (173) sky.

Collation: [unsigned 1–3⁸]; 24 leaves; unpaged, first and last leaves blank.

Contents: pp. 1–2: blank; p. 3: half title: 'The Ballad of the Burglar of Babylon'; pp. 4–5: title pages; p. 6: copyright page; p. 7: introduction; p. 8: blank; p. 9: half title; pp. 10–45: text; pp. 46–48: blank.

Paper and Binding: leaf measures 9¼ × 7¾ in. (239 × 196 mm.); yWhite (Centroid 92) wove paper; all edges trimmed; d. Yellow (85) endpapers; White (263) cloth cover stamped in d. Olive Brown (96) measures 9½ × 8⅙ in. (240 × 204 mm.); front cover: brownish Black (65) woodcut of the burglar hiding in lower right corner; spine: vertical, in brBlack, 'ELIZABETH BISHOP   The Ballad of the Burglar of Babylon FSG'.

Dust Jacket, by Ann Grifalconi: woodcut of buzzards, kite, and the burglar in d. Yellow (85), d. Olive Brown (96), and m. greenish Blue (173); front: '[in d.OlBr] By Elizabeth Bishop | [in Windsor outline type, in d.OlBr] The | Ballad of the | Burglar of | Babylon | [in d.OlBr] Woodcuts by | Ann Grifalconi'; spine: over the woodcut, in d.OlBr, 'ELIZABETH BISHOP The Ballad of the Burglar of Babylon Farrar, Straus & Giroux'; back: continuation of front woodcut; front flap: '$3.95 || *"The story of Micuçú is true,"* Eliza-|beth Bishop *writes in her foreword.* | *"It happened in Rio de Janeiro a few* | *years ago. . . . I was one of those* | *who watched the pursuit of Micuçú* | *through binoculars.* . . . *The rest of* | *the story is taken, often word for word,* | *from the daily papers, filled out by* | *what I know of the place and the* | *people.* | [¶]

A8

THE BALLAD OF THE BURGLAR OF | BABYLON—"a ballad as good as any | we have," according to *The New York* | *Review of Books*—tells the tragic story | of Micuçú, a young man who tried to | become a real gangster, like the ones | in the movies. He ends as "an enemy | of society," who would rather "settle | for ninety hours" hunted by police | and soldiers on the hill of Babylon | than the "ninety years they gave me." | [¶] Elizabeth Bishop's ballad of a | young criminal is illustrated by Ann | Grifalconi's dramatic, accurate wood-|cuts. || *all ages*'; back flap: 'ELIZABETH BISHOP'S *Poems*, a volume | which combines *North & South* and | *A Cold Spring*, was awarded the Pul-|itzer Prize in 1956. *Questions of* | *Travel*, another collection of poems, | followed in 1965. She has been de-|scribed as "one of the few true poets" | (Philip Booth, *The Christian Science* | *Monitor*) and "a poet pure and simple | who has perfect pitch" (Howard Moss, | *Kenyon Review*). Robert Lowell | writes, "When we read her, we enter | the classical serenity of a new country." | [¶] Miss Bishop has served as Poetry | Consultant to the Library of Congress | and is a member of the National Insti-|tute of Arts and Letters. From 1952 | to 1967 she lived in Brazil; at present | she is living in San Francisco. || ANN GRIFALCONI has made the pictures | for a number of outstanding books | for children, including Mary Hayes | Weik's *The Jazz Man*, which was an | ALA Notable Children's Book of 1966 | and which was chosen by *The New* | *York Times Book Review* as one of | the ten best-illustrated children's books | of that year. Miss Grifalconi wrote, as | well as illustrated, *City Rhythms*. She | lives in New York City. || FARRAR, STRAUS AND GIROUX | 19 UNION SQUARE WEST | NEW YORK 10003'.

Text Contents: introduction (signed "E.B."); "The Ballad of the Burglar of Babylon," originally "The Burglar of Babylon."

Publication: 10,400 copies published on April 23, 1968, at $3.95.

Locations: CWM, DLC, EB, MoSW (with dust jacket).

A9* *The Complete Poems.* Farrar, Straus and Giroux, New York, [n.d.] (spiral page proof)

[all on left margin] *Elizabeth Bishop* | [rule] | *The Complete Poems* | *Farrar, Straus and Giroux New York* | [publisher's device]

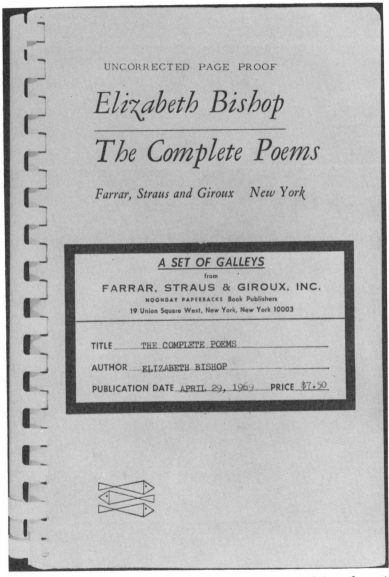

UNCORRECTED PAGE PROOF

Elizabeth Bishop

The Complete Poems

Farrar, Straus and Giroux   New York

A SET OF GALLEYS
from
FARRAR, STRAUS & GIROUX, INC.
NOONDAY PAPERBACKS Book Publishers
19 Union Square West, New York, New York 10003

TITLE___THE COMPLETE POEMS___

AUTHOR__ELIZABETH BISHOP___

PUBLICATION DATE_APRIL 29, 1969__ PRICE _$7.50_

A9* (proof cover)

Imprint: recto of first leaf, 'CRANE DUPLICATION SERVICES, INC. | on Cape Cod | Box 487, Barnstable, Massachusetts 02630 | Tel: 617–362–3441'.

Collation: 113 leaves; [1–2], [i–iv] v–viii, [1–2] 3–59 [60–62] 63–97 [98–102] 103–157 [158–160] 161–190 [191–192] 193–210 [211–216].

Contents: p. [1]: instructions: 'Attention, Reader!'; p. [2]: blank; p. i: half title: '*Elizabeth Bishop / The Complete Poems*'; p. ii: blank; p. iii: title page; p. iv: copyright page; pp. v–viii: contents; p. 1: half title: '*North & South*'; pp. 3–60: text; p. 61: half title and dedication: '*A Cold Spring* | TO DR. ANNY BAUMANN'; p. 62: blank; pp. 63–97: text; p. 98: blank; p. 99: half title and dedication: '*Questions of Travel* | FOR LOTA DE MACEDO SOARES | . . . *O dar-vos quanto tenho e quanto posso,* | *que quanto mais vos pago, mais vos devo.* | Camões'; p. 100: blank; p. 101: half title: 'Brazil'; p. 102: blank; pp. 103–140: text; p. 141: half title: 'Elsewhere'; p. 142: blank; pp. 143–158: text; p. 159: half title: '*Translations from the Portuguese*'; p. 160: blank; pp. 161–190: text; p. 191: half title: '*New and Uncollected Wrk*'; p. 192: blank; pp. 193–210: text; pp. 211–216: blank.

Paper and Binding: leaf measures 5½ × 8⅞₁₆ in. (214 × 139 mm.); yWhite (92) wove paper; all edges trimmed; stiff, l. greenish Yellow (101 close, no exact Centroid equivalent) unglazed paper with a White (263) plastic ring binding measures 8¼ × 6 in. (222 × 151 mm.); front: 'UNCORRECTED PAGE PROOF | *Elizabeth Bishop* | [rule] | *The Complete Poems* | *Farrar, Straus and Giroux New York* | [on a yWhite label edged and printed in d. Blue (183)] *A SET OF GALLEYS* | from | FARRAR, STRAUS & GIROUX, INC. | NOONDAY PAPERBACKS Book Publishers | 19 Union Square West, New York, New York 10003 | [rule] | TITLE [underlined information typed] THE COMPLETE POEMS | AUTHOR ELIZABETH BISHOP | PUBLICATION DATE APRIL 29, 1969 PRICE $7.50 | [beneath label, publisher's device]'; back: blank.

Text Contents: same as **A9**.

Location: CWM.

A9 *The Complete Poems.* Farrar, Straus and Giroux, New York, 1969
(first edition, first impression)

Elizabeth Bishop

The Complete Poems

Farrar, Straus and Giroux   New York

Title Page: 8⅜ × 6⅛ in. (212 × 155 mm.).

Thirty-two of the poems in this volume originally appeared in *The New Yorker* and six in *Poetry*. Certain poems were first published in *Direction, Forum, Harper's Bazaar, The Kenyon Review, Life and Letters Today, The Nation, New Democracy, New Directions in Prose and Poetry, The New Republic, The New York Review of Books, Partisan Review, The Quarterly Review of Literature, Saturday Review, Shenandoah, Trial Balances,* and *Vassar Review*.

Collation: [unsigned 1–7^{16}]; 112 leaves; [i–viii], [1–2] 3–59 [60–62] 63–97 [98–102] 103–157 [158–160] 161–190 [191–192] 193–210 [211] 212–213 [214] 215–216.

Contents: p. i: half title: 'Elizabeth Bishop / The Complete Poems'; p. ii: blank; p. iii: title page; p. iv: copyright page; p. v–viii: contents; p. 1: half title: 'North & South'; p. 2: blank; pp. 3–59: text; p. 60: blank; p. 61: half title and dedication: 'A Cold Spring | TO DR. ANNY BAUMANN'; p. 62: blank; pp. 63–97: text; p. 98: blank; p. 99: half title and dedication: 'Questions of Travel | FOR LOTA DE MACEDO SOARES | ... O dar-vos quanto tenho e quanto posso, | que quanto mais vos pago, mais vos *devo.* | Camões'; p. 100: blank; p. 101: half title: '*Brazil*' p. 102: blank; pp. 103–139: text; p. 140: blank; p. 141: half title: '*Elsewhere*'; p. 142: blank; pp. 143–157: text; p. 158: blank; p. 159: half title: '*Translations from the Portuguese*'; p. 160: blank; pp. 161–190: text; p. 191: half title: '*New and Uncollected Work*'; p. 192: blank; pp. 193–210: text; pp. 211–216: indexes.

Typography: text: 12/14 Linotype Granjon; display: Linotype Granjon and Monotype Garamond light; type page measures 180 × 110 mm., 27 lines of text per page.

Watermark: 'WARRENS OLDE STYLE'.

Paper and Binding: leaf measures 8⅜ × 6⅛ in. (212 × 155 mm.); yWhite (Centroid 92) laid paper; all edges trimmed, top edges stained v. Yellow (82); grayish Blue (186.5) wove endpapers; unglazed d. Blue (183) cloth cover measures 8¾ × 6⁵⁄₁₆ in. (220 × 158 mm.); spine: '[in gold] *Elizabeth* | *Bishop* | [rule] | *The* | *Complete* | *Poems* | [impressed only: publisher's device] | [in gold] *Farrar* | *Straus* | *and* | *Giroux*'.

Dust Jacket, by Roxanne Cumming: White (263), d. Blue (183 close, but no exact Centroid equivalent), Black (267), v. Yellow (82, close, but no exact Centroid equivalent), in an uneven stripe; front: in Black on White, '*Elizabeth Bishop / The Complete Poems*'; on spine: '[in Black on White] *Elizabeth* | *Bishop* | [rule] | *The* | *Complete* | *Poems* | [in White on d.B] *Farrar,* | *Straus* | *and* | *Giroux* | [publisher's device]'; back: '[in Black on White] "I am sure no living poet is as curious and observant as Miss Bishop. | What cuts so deeply is that each poem is inspired by her own tone, a | tone of large, grave tenderness and sorrowing amusement. She is too | sure of herself for empty mastery and breezy plagiarism, too interested | for confession and musical monotony, too powerful for mismanaged | fire, and too civilized for idiosyncratic incoherence. She has a humor-|ous, commanding genius for picking up the unnoticed, now making | something sprightly and right, and now a great monument. Once her | poems, each shining, were too few. Now they are many. When we | read her, we enter the classical serenity of a new country." | —*Robert Lowell* || [in White on d.B] "Elizabeth Bishop's poems are quiet, truthful, sad, funny, most | marvelously individual poems; they have a sound, a feel, a whole | moral

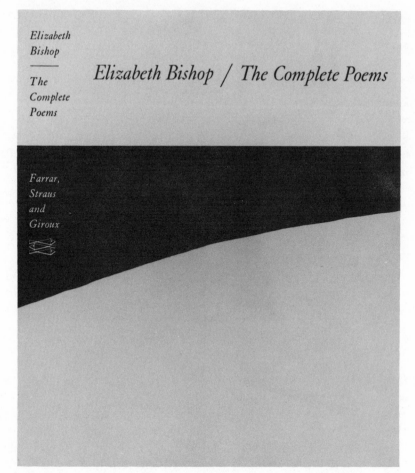

*Elizabeth
Bishop*

———

*The
Complete
Poems*

Elizabeth Bishop / The Complete Poems

*Farrar,
Straus
and
Giroux*

A9

and physical atmosphere, different from anything else I know. | They
are honest, modest, minutely observant, masterly; even their most |
complicated or troubled or imaginative effects seem, always, personal |
and natural, and as unmistakable as the first few notes of a Mahler |
song, the first few patches of a Vuillard interior. Her best poems—
| poems like 'The Man-Moth,' 'The Fish,' 'The Weed,' 'Roosters,' 'The
| Prodigal Son,' 'Faustina, or Rock Roses,' 'The Armadillo"—remind |
one of Vuillard or even, sometimes, of Vermeer. . . . The more you |
read her poems, the better and fresher, the more nearly perfect | they
seem." | —*Randall Jarrell*'; front flap: '$7.50 || *Elizabeth Bishop* |
[rule] | *The Complete Poems* || This volume gathers the poetry—work
of | three decades—by one of the master poets of | the age. | [¶]In

1955 Elizabeth Bishop was awarded the | Pulitzer Prize for the com-
bined edition of | *North & South* and *A Cold Spring*, a volume |
Randall Jarrell called "one of the best books | an American poet has
written." In this book | *North & South* and *A Cold Spring* are |
followed by her subsequent collection, | *Questions of Travel* (1965),
excepting the | story "In the Village," which Miss Bishop is |
reserving for a future collection of her fiction. | There is a group of
translations of two | contemporary Brazilian poets, Carlos
Drum-|mond de Andrade and João Cabral de Melo | Neto. And the
book concludes with a group | of Miss Bishop's own distinctive poems,
all | previously uncollected. || *Farrar, Straus and Giroux* | 19 UNION
SQUARE WEST | NEW YORK 10003'; back flap: ' "Miss Bishop
looks at, and into, the world | with an eye so individual that to share her
| vision is—gratefully—to revise one's own. . . . | She is one of the few
true poets of this, or | any, hemisphere." | —*Philip Booth* || "Eliza-
beth Bishop subscribes to no schools or | theories, though you might say
that she is a | school in herself of the schooled diction, the | schooled
eye. . . . She came upon her way | of seeing things years ago. One may
talk or | not about the, as it were, method—i.e., the | organization of
off-beat, penetrating insights | —but it remains, like all original things,
| inimitable. The mad exactness of the nota-|tion is nearly always both
disturbing and | exciting because it is so purified, discreet, and | yet
rash. In a sense she takes no chances | and yet by her raffish connections
she is of the | sort to take every chance. . . . Having one of | the least
conventional points of view, it is | her strength to make the freshness
seem | inevitable." | —*Jean Garrigue* || "What Elizabeth Bishop
brings to poetry is | a new imagination: because of that, she is |
revolutionary, not 'experimental.' . . . Ad-|mired by critics, poets, and
anyone genuinely | interested in writing, her work is not easily |
labeled. . . . She is not academic, beat, | cooked, raw, formal, informal,
metrical, | syllabic, or what have you. She is a poet pure | and simple
who has perfect pitch." | —*Howard Moss* || *Jacket design by Roxanne
Cumming*'.

Text Contents: North & South, reprinted with added dedications: "Quai
d'Orleans (for Margaret Miller)"; "Little Exercise (for Thomas Ed-
wards Wanning)"; "Anaphora (in memory of Marjorie Carr Stevens)";
A Cold Spring, reprinted from the 1955 edition, without "Arrival at
Santos" and "The Mountain" and with a dedication, "for Louise
Crane," added to "Letter to N.Y."; *Questions of Travel*, reprinted from

the 1965 edition, with "Arrival at Santos" and without "In the Village"; translations from the Portuguese: Carlos Drummond de Andrade's "Seven-Sided Poem," "Travelling in the Family," and "The Table" and portions of João Cabral de Melo Neto's *The Death and Life of a Severino*; new and uncollected work: "Rainy Season; Sub-Tropics: Giant Toad, Strayed Crab, and Giant Snail," "The Hanging of the Mouse," "Some Dreams They Forgot," "Song," "House Guest," "Trouvée (for Mr. Wheaton Galentine and Mr. Harold Leeds)," "Going to the Bakery," "Under the Window: Ouro Preto (for Lilli Correia de Araújo)."

Publication: first printing: 5,500 copies published on April 29, 1969, at $7.50; second printing: 4,000 copies, 1970 (in paper); third printing: 3,000 copies in paper and 2,000 copies in cloth, 1970; fourth printing: 1,500 copies, 1975 (in paper); fifth printing: 1,544 copies, March 1977 (in paper); sixth printing: 3,579 copies (in paper).

Locations: CWM, DLC (deposit copies stamped 22 April 1969 and 19 May 1969, 3 copies), EB, MoSW (with dust jacket), TxR, TxU.

A9.a2   *The Complete Poems.* Second printing, 1970 (first edition, second impression, from letterpress plates, paperback, perfect bound)

Elizabeth Bishop | [rule] | *The Complete Poems* | *Farrar, Straus and Giroux New York* | [publisher's device]

Copyright © 1933, 1935, 1936, 1937, 1938, 1939, 1940, 1941, 1944, 1945, 1946, 1947, 1948, 1949, 1951, 1952, 1955, 1956, 1957, 1958, 1959, 1960, 1961, 1962, 1963, 1964, 1965, 1966, 1967, 1968, 1969 by Elizabeth Bishop.
Library of Congress catalog card number: 69-15407
All rights reserved
Printed in the United States of America by
American Book-Stratford Press, Inc.
Published simultaneously in Canada by
Doubleday Canada Ltd., Toronto
Second Printing, 1970
Designed by Cynthia Muser

Thirty-two of the poems in this volume originally appeared in *The New Yorker* and six in *Poetry.* Certain poems were first published in *Direction, Forum, Harper's Bazaar, The Kenyon Review, Life and Letters Today, The Nation, New Democracy, New Directions in Prose and Poetry, The New Republic, The New York Review of Books, Partisan Review, The Quarterly Review of Literature, Saturday Review, Shenandoah, Trial Balances,* and *Vassar Review.*

Collation: same as **A9**.

Contents: same as **A9** with the exception of the format of the copyright

Sunburst 10

ELIZABETH
BISHOP

THE
COMPLETE
POEMS

$2.95

A9.a2

page. Despite the changed appearance of the page, only one thing has been added: the American printer has incorporated.

Typography: same as **A9**.

Paper and Binding: leaf and paper wrapper measure 8¼ × 5⅜ in. (210 × 138 mm.); yWhite (Centroid 92) wove paper; all edges trimmed; stiff, glazed White (263) paper wrapper; front wrapper: '[s. yellowish Green (131)] Sunburst 10 | [in Black (267)] *ELIZABETH* | *BISH-OP* | [s.yG, l. greenish Yellow (101), Black, l. Gray (264) sunburst design] | [in Black] *THE* | *COMPLETE* | *POEMS* | [in s.yG] $2.95'; spine: '[vertical, in Black] *Elizabeth Bishop* / *The Complete Poems* [horizontal, in s.yG sunburst device] [in Black] S 10'; back wrapper: '[in s.yG] *SUNBURST BOOKS* [in Black] *presents the essential writings of* | [nine lines in Black describing Sunburst Books] || [a description of ten titles, 20 lines in Black] || [in Black] *Design by Patricia de Groot* || [in s.yG] SUNBURST BOOKS | [in Black] A Division of FARRAR, STRAUS & GIROUX | 19 Union Square West | New York 10003'.

Text Contents: same as **A9**.

Publication: 4,000 copies in 1970, at $2.95.

Locations: CWM, MoSW.

A9.[a6] *The Complete Poems*. Sixth printing, 1978 (first edition, eighth impression, from offset plates from the first edition, paperback, Smyth sewn)

Elizabeth Bishop | [rule] | *The Complete Poems* | *Farrar, Straus and Giroux New York* | [publisher's device]

> *Copyright* © *1933, 1935, 1936, 1937, 1938, 1939, 1940, 1941, 1944, 1945, 1946, 1947, 1948, 1949, 1951, 1952, 1955, 1956, 1957, 1958, 1959, 1960, 1961, 1962, 1963, 1964, 1965, 1966, 1967, 1968, 1969 by Elizabeth Bishop.*
> *Library of Congress catalog card number: 69–15407*
> *All rights reserved*
> *Printed in the United States of America*
> *Published simultaneously in Canada*
> *First printing, 1969*
> *Designed by Cynthia Muser*
> *Sixth printing, 1978*
>
> Thirty-two of the poems in this volume originally appeared in *The New Yorker* and six in *Poetry*. Certain poems were first published in *Direction, Forum, Harper's Bazaar, The Kenyon Review, Life and Letters Today, The Nation, New Democracy, New Directions in Prose and Poetry, The New Republic, The New York Review of Books, Partisan Review, The Quarterly Review of Literature, Saturday Review, Shenandoah, Trial Balances,* and *Vassar Review*.

Collation: same as **A9**.

Contents: same as **A9** with the exception of the copyright notice. The names of the American printer and Canadian publisher have been deleted, and the date of the first printing has been added.

Typography: same as **A9**.

Paper and Binding: leaf and stiff, glazed paper wrapper measure 8⅜ × 6⅛ in. (214 × 156 mm.); yWhite (Centroid 92) wove paper; all edges trimmed; design similar to the design of the dust jacket of **A9**; front wrapper: same as dust jacket of **A9**; spine: '[vertical, in Black (267) on White (263)] *Elizabeth Bishop* [in White on d. Blue (183 close, no exact Centroid equivalent)] *The Complete Poems* [in Black on v. Yellow (182 close, no exact Centroid equivalent), publisher's device] [horizontal, in Black on v.Y] N 613'; back wrapper: same quotes by Robert Lowell and Randall Jarrell as on the jacket of **A9** and '[in White on d.B] *Cover design by Roxanne Cumming* || Farrar, Straus and Giroux | 19 Union Square West | New York 10003 | ISBN 0-374-51516-6 | $5.95 [in Black on v.Y] *National Book Award for Poetry*'.

Text Contents: same as **A9**.

Publication: 3,579 copies in October 1978, at $5.95.

Location: CWM.

Note: the fifth printing was the first to be Smyth sewn.

"I am sure no living poet is as curious and observant as Miss Bishop. What cuts so deeply is that each poem is inspired by her own tone, a tone of large, grave tenderness and sorrowing amusement. She is too sure of herself for empty mastery and breezy plagiarism, too interested for confession and musical monotony, too powerful for mismanaged fire, and too civilized for idiosyncratic incoherence. She has a humorous, commanding genius for picking up the unnoticed, now making something sprightly and right, and now a great monument. Once her poems, each shining, were too few. Now they are many. When we read her, we enter the classical serenity of a new country."

—*Robert Lowell*

"Elizabeth Bishop's poems are quiet, truthful, sad, funny, most marvelously individual poems; they have a sound, a feel, a whole moral and physical atmosphere, different from anything else I know. They are honest, modest, minutely observant, masterly; even their most complicated or troubled or imaginative effects seem, always, personal and natural, and as unmistakable as the first few notes of a Mahler song, the first few patches of a Vuillard interior. Her best poems—poems like 'The Man-Moth,' 'The Fish,' 'The Weed,' 'Roosters,' 'The Prodigal Son,' 'Faustina, or Rock Roses,' 'The Armadillo"—remind one of Vuillard or even, sometimes, of Vermeer.... The more you read her poems, the better and fresher, the more nearly perfect they seem."

—*Randall Jarrell*

Cover design by Roxanne Cumming

Farrar, Straus and Giroux
19 Union Square West
New York 10003

ISBN 0-374-51516-6

$5.95

National Book Award for Poetry

A9.[a6]

A9.[b1] *The Complete Poems.* Chatto and Windus, London, [1970]
(first edition, third impression, produced by offset)

Elizabeth Bishop

The Complete Poems

Chatto and Windus · London

Title Page: 8⁷⁄₁₆ × 6⅛ in. (213.5 × 155.5 mm.).

Collation: [unsigned 1–14⁸]; 112 leaves; [i–viii], [1–2] 3–59 [60–62] 63–97[98–102] 103–157 [158–160] 161–190 [191–192] 193–210 [211] 212–213 [214] 215–216.

Contents: same as **A9**.

Typography: same as **A9**.

Paper and Binding: leaf measures 8⁷⁄₁₆ × 6⅛ in. (213.5 × 155.5 mm.); yWhite (Centroid 92) laid paper; all edges trimmed, top edges unstained in contrast to **A9**; yWhite wove endpapers; unglazed deep Blue (179) cloth cover measures 8¹¹⁄₁₆ × 6⁵⁄₁₆ in. (220 × 160 mm.); spine: in gold, '*Elizabeth* | *Bishop* | [rule] | *The* | *Complete* | *Poems* | *Chatto* | *and* | *Windus*'.

Dust Jacket, by Roxanne Cumming: same as **A9** except for the flaps. Six lines and the price are added to the front flap: '*Winner of the National Book Award* | *Jacket design by Roxanne Cumming* | ISBN 0 7011 1608 0 | £2.25 | 45s | net'. The back flap is entirely different: '*Elizabeth Bishop* | *Selected Poems* || "... the exultation of high art, the authentic | *frisson.* Serene, lovely, 'curious and observant', | she shows undiminished mastery; 'Manuel-|zinho' is masterly; nothing is less than enjoyable." | —MAURICE WIGGIN || "This highly respected American poet is | discriminating, witty, precise, fastidious, but | above all she knows the look and feel of things | and the way they enter our lives.... One is first | struck by the magnificent surfaces of her | poems; later one sees that the point is to feel | something else underlying the descriptions and | lending them an air of dream, despite (and | perhaps because of) their clarity." | —MARTIN DODSWORTH || "A curious and passionate observer, with a | magic gift for the odd and piquant detail.... | Her best manner is sprightly and thoughtful. | Her subjects are drawn from travel over three | continents.... The kind of wonder she finds | in the eye of a little tin horse ('Cirque | d'Hiver') or in the seal with its 'sort of shrug' | ('At the Fishhouses') bursts through again and | again with a quick and often metaphysical | fire." | —*The Times* || 21s(£1.05) net || CHATTO & WINDUS LTD | *42 William IV Street London WC2*'.

Text Contents: same as **A9**.

Publication: first printing: 1,000 copies published on October 29, 1970; second printing: 1,000 copies, March 1971.

Locations: BL (deposit copy stamped 27 October 1970), DLC, EB, MoSW (with dust jacket).

Note: on the second impression there is a change of printer:
    Imprint: on verso of title page, 'Reproduced and printed in Great Britain | by Redwood Press Limited, | Trowbridge and London'.

A9.[b1]

A10 *An Anthology of Twentieth-Century Brazilian Poetry*, ed. with Emanuel Brasil. Wesleyan University Press, Middletown, Connecticut, 1972 (first edition, first impression, cloth and paperback, perfect bound)

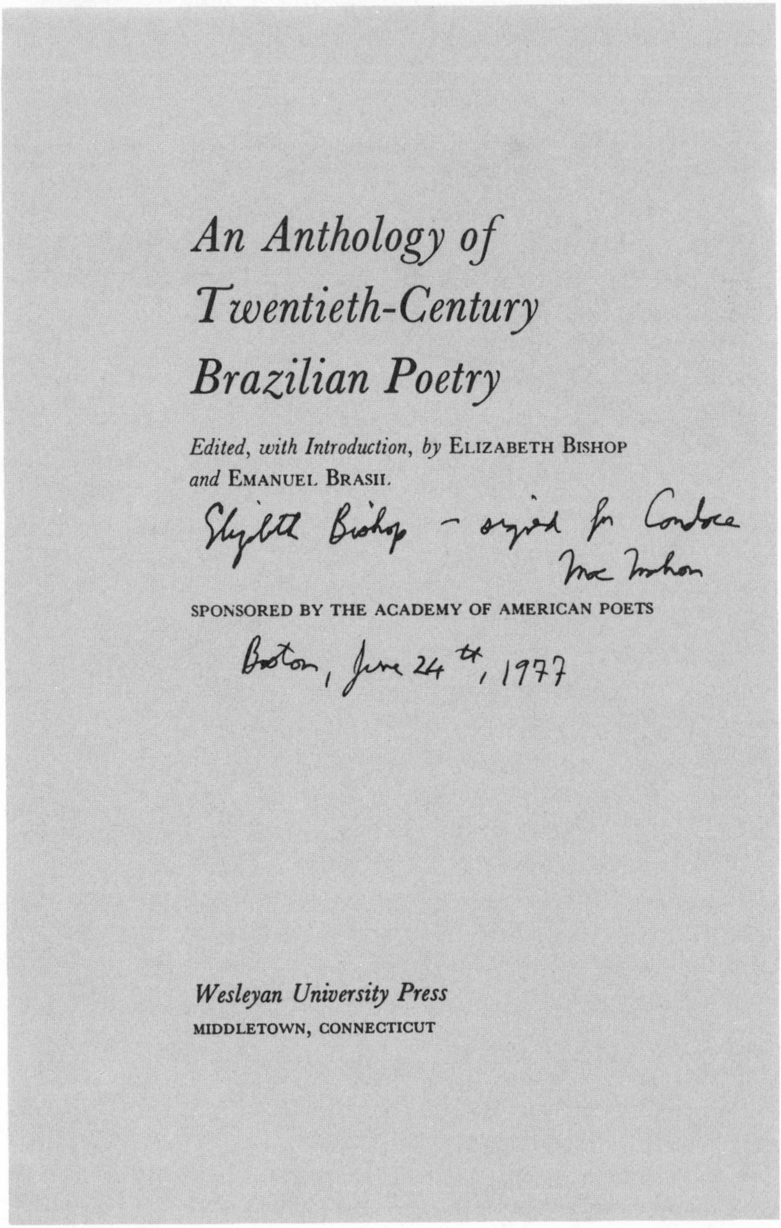

An Anthology of Twentieth-Century Brazilian Poetry

Edited, with Introduction, by ELIZABETH BISHOP *and* EMANUEL BRASIL.

[handwritten: Elizabeth Bishop — signed for Candace Mac Mahon]

SPONSORED BY THE ACADEMY OF AMERICAN POETS

[handwritten: Boston, June 24th, 1977]

Wesleyan University Press
MIDDLETOWN, CONNECTICUT

Title Page: 9 × 5¹⁵/₁₆ in. (228 × 151 mm.).

Clothbound ISBN: 0-8195-4044-7

Paperbound ISBN: 0-8195-6023-5

Library of Congress catalog card number: 75-184359

Manufactured in the United States of America

FIRST EDITION

Collation: [unsigned 1–3^{16} 4^8 5–7^{16}]; 104 leaves; blank leaf, [i–vi] vii–xi [xii] xiii–xxi [xxii], [1] 2–181 [182–184].

Contents: blank leaf; p. i: half title: '*An Anthology of Twentieth-Century | Brazilian Poetry*'; p. ii: blank; p. iii: title page; p. iv: copyright page; p. v: dedication: 'To the memory of MANUEL BANDEIRA'; p. vi: blank; pp. vii–xi: '*Contents*'; p. xii: blank; p. xiii–xxi: '*Introduction*'; p. xxii: blank; p. 1: half title; p. 2–173: text: '*Manuel Bandeira*', pp. 2–9; '*Oswald de Andrade*', pp. 10–17; '*Jorge de Lima*', pp. 18–19; '*Mário de Andrade*', pp. 20–23; '*Cassiano Ricardo*', pp. 24–27; '*Joaquim Cardozo*', pp. 28–33; '*Cecília Meireles*', pp. 34–47; '*Murilo Mendes*', pp. 48–55; '*Carlos Drummond de Andrade*', pp. 56–93; '*Vinícius de Moraes*' pp.

94–111; 'Mauro Mota', pp. 112–113; 'João Cabral de Melo Neto', pp. 114–165; 'Marcos Konder Reis', pp. 166–169; 'Ferreira Gullar', pp. 170–173; p. 174: blank; pp. 175–177: 'Bibliography'; p. 178: blank; pp. 179–181: 'Notes on Editors and Translators'; blank leaf.

Typography: text: 11/13 Baskerville; display: Monotype Baskerville; type page measures 186 × 111 mm., 41 lines per page.

Paper and Binding (Cloth Edition): leaf measures 9 × 5¹⁵⁄₁₆ in. (228 × 151 mm.); yWhite (Centroid 92) wove paper; all edges trimmed; d. greenish Yellow (103) endpapers; d. Blue (183) unglazed cloth cover measures 9³⁄₁₆ × 6³⁄₁₆ in. (233 × 157 mm.); spine: in silver, '[vertical] An Anthology of Twentieth-Century | Brazilian Poetry | [horizontal] Edited by | BISHOP | & | BRASIL | * | WESLEYAN'.

Dust Jacket: front: on deep greenish Yellow (100), in Black (267) and White (263), 'MANUEL BANDEIRA * OSWALD de ANDRADE | JORGE de LIMA * MÁRIO de ANDRADE * | CASSIANO RICARDO * JOAQUIM CARDOZO | CECÍLIA MEIRELES * MURILO MENDES * CARLOS | DRUMMOND de ANDRADE * VINÍCIUS de MORAES | MAURO MOTA * JOÃO CABRAL de MELO NETO | MARCOS KONDER REIS * FERREIRA GULLAR | AN ANTHOLOGY OF TWENTIETH-CEN-TURY | BRAZILIAN POETRY | Edited, with Introduction, by ELIZABETH BISHOP and | EMANUEL BRASIL; with transla-tions by ELIZABETH | BISHOP * PAUL BLACKBURN * ASH-LEY BROWN * | JANE COOPER * RICHARD EBERHART * BAR-|BARA HOWES * JUNE JORDAN * GALWAY KINNELL | JEAN LONGLAND * JAMES MERRILL * W. S. MERWIN | LOUIS SIMPSON * MARK STRAND * JEAN VALEN-|TINE * RICHARD WILBUR * JAMES WRIGHT'; spine: '[vertical, in White] AN ANTHOLOGY OF TWENTIETH-CENTURY | BRAZILIAN POETRY | [horizontal, in Black] Edited by | BISHOP | & | BRASIL | [in White] * | [in Black] WESLEYAN'; back: same as front; front flap: on White in d. Blue (183), '$11.00 | [¶] This bilingual anthology, published | under the sponsorship of The Aca-demy | of American Poets, presents representa-|tive poems, with English translations | en face, | from the work of fourteen Brazilian poets of the "Modern Genera-|tion" and of the "Post-War Genera-|tion" of 1945: Manuel Bandeira, | Oswald de Andrade, Jorge de Lima, | Mário de Andrade, Cassiano Ricardo, | Joaquim Cardozo,

MANUEL BANDEIRA ∗ OSWALD de ANDRADE

JORGE de LIMA ∗ MÁRIO de ANDRADE ∗

CASSIANO RICARDO ∗ JOAQUIM CARDOZO

CECÍLIA MEIRELES ∗ MURILO MENDES ∗ CARLOS

DRUMMOND de ANDRADE ∗ VINÍCIUS de MORAES

MAURO MOTA ∗ JOÃO CABRAL de MELO NETO

MARCOS KONDER REIS ∗ FERREIRA GULLAR

AN ANTHOLOGY OF TWENTIETH-CENTURY

BRAZILIAN POETRY

Edited, with Introduction, by ELIZABETH BISHOP and

EMANUEL BRASIL; with translations by ELIZABETH

BISHOP ∗ PAUL BLACKBURN ∗ ASHLEY BROWN ∗

JANE COOPER ∗ RICHARD EBERHART ∗ BAR-

BARA HOWES ∗ JUNE JORDAN ∗ GALWAY KINNELL

JEAN LONGLAND ∗ JAMES MERRILL ∗ W. S. MERWIN

LOUIS SIMPSON ∗ MARK STRAND ∗ JEAN VALEN-

TINE ∗ RICHARD WILBUR ∗ JAMES WRIGHT

Edited by
BISHOP
&
BRASIL

WESLEYAN

A10

Cecília Meireles, | Murilo Mendes, Carlos Drummond de | Andrade, Vinícius de Moraes, Mauro | Mota, João Cabral de Melo Neto, | Marcos Konder Reis, and Ferreira | Gullar. | [¶] In Brazil, despite widespread il-|literacy and the lack of a truly modern | system of communications, poets and | poetry are highly esteemed. Indeed, | *poeta* is sometimes used as a compli-|mentary name or a term of affection, | even though the person so called may | be a businessman or a politician. But | few North Americans know anything | about the lively, colorful, intrinsically | musical poetry of Brazil, just as they |

know so little else about their large | southern neighbor. The purpose of this | collection is to introduce the North || *(continued on back flap)*'; back flap: '*(continued from front flap)* || American reader to the four-teen poets | represented, probably the best known | and the best loved poets of their | country. || [publisher's device] | [in d. greenish Yellow (103) *Wesleyan University Press* | MIDDLETOWN, CON-NECTICUT'.

Paper and Binding (Paper Edition): leaf and paper wrapper measure 8¹⁵⁄₁₆ × 5⅞ in. (228 × 150 mm.); yWhite (Centroid 92) laid paper, all edges trimmed; stiff, unglazed, m. Olive (107) paper wrapper; front and spine exactly the same as the dust jacket of the cloth edition; back: on White in d. Blue (183), 'POETRY / 623 | This bilingual anthology, published under the sponsorship of The | Academy of American Poets, presents representative poems, with | English translations *en face*, from the work of fourteen Brazilian | poets of the "Modern Generation" and of the "Post-War Genera-|tion" of 1945: Manuel Bandeira, Oswald de Andrade, Jorge de | Lima, Mário de Andrade, Cassiano Ricardo, Joaquim Cardozo, | Cecília Meireles, Murilo Mendes, Carlos Drum-mond de Andrade, | Vinícius de Moraes, Mauro Mota, João Cabral de Melo Neto, | Marcos Konder Reis, and Ferreira Gullar. | [¶] In Brazil, despite widespread illiteracy and the lack of | a truly modern system of communications, poets and poetry | are highly esteemed. Indeed, *poeta* is sometimes used as a | complimentary name or a term of affection, even though the | person so called may be a businessman or a politician. But | few North Americans know anything about the lively, colorful, | intrinsically musical poetry of Brazil, just as they know so | little else about their large southern neighbor. The purpose | of this collection is to introduce the North American reader | to the fourteen poets represented, probably the best known | and the best loved of their country. | [m.Ol rule] | [publisher's device] *This book is also available in a clothbound edition* | Wesleyan University Press | MIDDLE-TOWN, CONNECTICUT 06457 | $3.45 | ISBN: 0-8195-6023-5 | Printed in U. S. A.'

Text Contents: an Introduction by EB and Emanuel Brasil and translations by EB of these poems: Manuel Bandeira, "O Último Poema / My (The) Last Poem," pp. 2–3, "Tragédia Brasileira / Brazilian Tragedy," pp. 8–9; Joaquim Cardozo, "Cemitério da Infância / Ce-metery of Childhood," pp. 28–31; Carlos Drummond de Andrade,

"Viagem Na Família / Travelling in the Family," pp. 56–61, "Poemâ de Sete Faces / Seven-Sided Poem," pp. 62–63, "Não Se Mate / Don't Kill Yourself," pp. 64–65, "A Mesa / The Table," pp. 66–83, "Infância / Infancy," pp. 84–87, "No Meio do Caminho / In the Middle of the Road," pp. 88–89; "Retrato de Família / Family Portrait," pp. 90–93; Vinícius Moraes, "Sonêto de Intimidade / Sonnet of Intimacy," pp. 102–103; João Cabral de Melo Neto, "Morte e Vida Severina (O Retirante) / The Death and Life of a Severino (The 'Retirante')," pp. 126–129, "Morte e Vida Severina (Encontra dois . . .) / The Death and Life of a Severino (He meets . . .)," pp. 130–137, "Morte e Vida Severina (Aparacem e se . . .) / The Death and Life of a Severino (Neighbors, friends . . .)," pp. 138–139.

Publication: first printing: 2,000 copies in cloth, at $11.00, and 2,500 copies in paper, at $3.45, on April 13, 1972; second printing: 3,000 copies, 1974 (in paper).

Locations: CWM, DLC (deposit copy stamped 24 May 1972), EB, MoSW (with jacket and in paper), TxR.

A11   *Poem*. The Phoenix Book Shop, New York, 1973 (first edition, first impression)

Elizabeth Bishop

Poem

THE PHOENIX BOOK SHOP
New York
1973

Title Page: 7 × 5 in. (178 × 127 mm.).

Copyright © 1972 by Elizabeth Bishop

*Acknowledgment is made to the New Yorker
where this poem first appeared.*

Colophon: p. [13]: 'This first edition of Poem | is limited to twenty-six copies lettered A to Z, | not for sale, and one hundred copies | numbered and signed by the author. | This is no. 16 in the Phoenix Book Shop | Oblong Octavo Series. | Copy no. | [signature]'. Copy numbers were handwritten in red ink.

Imprint: p. [14]: 'Designed and printed at the Ferguson Press, Cambridge, Mass.'

A11

Collation: [unsigned 1⁸]; unpaged.

Contents: p. 1–2: blank; p. 3: title page; p. 4: copyright page; p. 5: half title, 'POEM'; p. 6: blank; p. 7–11: text: p. 12: blank; p. 13: signature; p. 14: colophon; pp. 15–16: blank.

Paper and Binding: leaf measures 7×5 in. (178×127 mm.); yWhite (Centroid 92) laid paper; all edges trimmed; unglazed marbleized paper wrapper, v.d. greenish Blue (175), deep Blue (179), and v. deep Red (14) measures 7 5/16 × 5 9/16 in. (187×140 mm.); front wrapper: in Black (267), centered on glued yWhite paper rectangle, 'Poem | Elizabeth Bishop'.

Text Contents: "Poem."

Publication: 126 copies on April 17, 1973, at $15.00.

Locations: CWM (copy No. 20), DLC (no deposit stamp, copy No. 7), EB, MoSW (two copies), TxU.

A12 *Poems.* Speculum Musicae, New York, 1976 (first edition, first impression)

Young Concert Artists presents
SPECULUM MUSICAE
February 24, 1976

Poems　　*Elizabeth Bishop*　　*Farrar, Straus and Giroux*

ANAPHORA

in memory of Marjorie Carr Stevens

Each day with so much ceremony
begins, with birds, with bells,
with whistles from a factory;
such white-gold skies our eyes
first open on, such brilliant walls
that for a moment we wonder
"Where is the music coming from, the energy?
The day was meant for what ineffable creature
we must have missed?" Oh promptly he
appears and takes his earthly nature
　　instantly, instantly falls
　　victim of long intrigue,
　　assuming memory and mortal
　　mortal fatigue.

More slowly falling into sight
and showering into stippled faces,
darkening, condensing all his light;
in spite of all the dreaming
squandered upon him with that look,
suffers our uses and abuses,
sinks through the drift of bodies,
sinks through the drift of classes
to evening to the beggar in the park
who, weary, without lamp or book
　　prepares stupendous studies:
　　the fiery event
　　of every day in endless
　　endless assent.

ARGUMENT

Days that cannot bring you near
or will not,
Distance trying to appear
something more than obstinate,
argue argue argue with me
endlessly
neither proving you less wanted nor less dear.

Distance: Remember all that land
beneath the plane;
that coastline
of dim beaches deep in sand
stretching indistinguishably
all the way,
all the way to where my reasons end?

Days: And think
of all those cluttered instruments,
one to a fact,
canceling each other's experience;
how they were
like some hideous calendar
"Compliments of Never & Forever, Inc."

The intimidating sound
of these voices
we must separately find

can and shall be vanquished:
Days and Distance disarrayed again
and gone
both for good and from the gentle battleground.

recto

Broadside: 11 × 8½ in. (279 × 215 mm.)

SANDPIPER

The roaring alongside he takes for granted,
and that every so often the world is bound to shake.
He runs, he runs to the south, finical, awkward,
in a state of controlled panic. a student of Blake.

The beach hisses like fat. On his left, a sheet
of interrupting water comes and goes
and glazes over his dark and brittle feet.
He runs, he runs straight through it, watching his toes.

—Watching. rather, the spaces of sand between them,
where (no detail too small) the Atlantic drains
rapidly backwards and downwards. As he runs,
he stares at the dragging grains.

The world is a mist. And then the world is
minute and vast and clear. The tide
is higher or lower. He couldn't tell you which.
His beak is focussed; he is preoccupied,

looking for something, something, something.
Poor bird, he is obsessed!
The millions of grains are black, white, tan, and gray,
mixed with quartz grains, rose and amethyst.

INSOMNIA

The moon in the bureau mirror
looks out a million miles
(and perhaps with pride, at herself,
but she never, never smiles)
far and away beyond sleep, or
perhaps she's a daytime sleeper.

By the Universe deserted,
she'd tell it to go to hell,
and she'd find a body of water,
or a mirror, on which to dwell.
So wrap up care in a cobweb
and drop it down the well

into that world inverted
where left is always right,
where the shadows are really the body,
where we stay awake all night,
where the heavens are shallow as the sea
is now deep, and you love me.

VIEW OF THE CAPITOL
FROM THE LIBRARY OF CONGRESS

Moving from left to left, the light
is heavy on the Dome, and coarse.
One small lunette turns it aside
and blankly stares off to the side
like a big white old wall-eyed horse.

On the east steps the Air Force Band
in uniforms of Air Force blue
is playing hard and loud, but—queer—
the music doesn't quite come through.

It comes in snatches, dim then keen,
then mute, and yet there is no breeze.
The giant trees stand in between.
I think the trees must intervene,

catching the music in their leaves
like gold-dust, till each big leaf sags.
Unceasingly the little flags
feed their limp stripes into the air,
and the band's efforts vanish there.

Great shades, edge over,
give the music room.
The gathered brasses want to go
boom—boom.

O Breath

Beneath that loved   and celebrated breast,
silent, bored really   blindly veined,
grieves, maybe   lives and lets
live, passes   bets,
something moving   but invisibly,
and with what clamor   why restrained
I cannot fathom   even a ripple.
(See the thin flying   of nine black hairs
four around one   five the other nipple,
flying almost intolerably   on your own breath.)
Equivocal, but what we have in common's   bound to be there,
whatever we must own   equivalents for,
something that maybe I   could bargain with
and make a separate peace   beneath
within   if never with.

verso

Collation: broadside.

Contents: six poems selected by Elliot Carter for "A Mirror on Which to Dwell" (**F3**). Recto: "Anaphora" and "Argument;" verso: "Sandpiper," "View of the Capitol from the Library of Congress," "Insomnia," and "O Breath."

Paper and Typography: 11 × 8½ in. (279 × 215 mm.); White (263) unglazed paper. Probably reproduced photographically from the individual poems and the title page display of **A9**.

Publication: distributed with programs at the first performance of "A Mirror on Which to Dwell," February 24, 1976.

Note: Later issues are undated and have been distributed at all subsequent performances. They have only a title, *Elizabeth Bishop/Poems*, from the half title of **A9**.

A13   *Geography III*. Farrar, Straus and Giroux, New York, 1976 (first
edition, first impression)

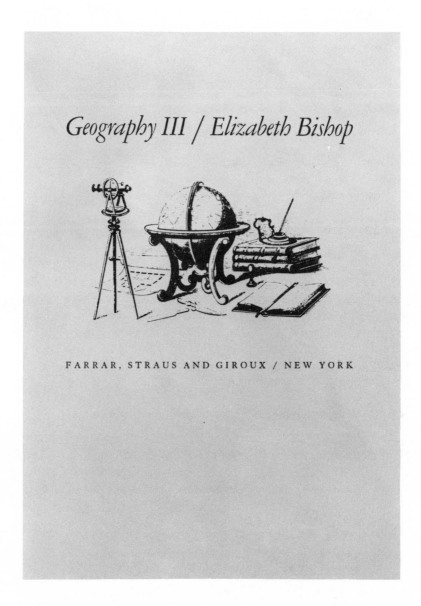

Title Page: 8½ × 6⅛ in. (215 × 156 mm.).

Collation: [unsigned 1–2¹⁶]; 32 leaves; [x–xii], [1–2] 3–50 [51–52].

Contents: p. i: blank; p. ii: '*Books by Elizabeth Bishop* | *North & South* | *A Cold Spring* | *Questions of Travel* | *The Complete Poems* | *Geography III* | *The Diary of "Helena Morley"* (*translator*) | *Contemporary Brazilian Poetry* (*co-editor*)' p. iii: half title: '*Geography III*'; p. iv: blank; p. v: title page; p. vi: copyright page; p. vii: dedication: '*For Alice Methfessel*'; p. viii: blank; p. ix: contents; pp. x–xi: epigraph; p. xii: blank; p. 1: half title; p. 2: blank; pp. 3–50: text; pp. 51–52: blank.

Typography: text: 12/16 Linotype Granjon; display: Linotype Granjon and Ludlow Garamond; type page measures 157 × 102 mm., 21 lines of text per page.

Paper and Binding: leaf measures 8½ × 6⅛ in. (215 × 156 mm.); yWhite (Centroid 92) wove paper; all edges trimmed; l. yellowish Brown (76.5 close, no exact Centroid equivalent) endpapers; unglazed grayish Brown (61) cloth cover measures 8¾ × 6⅜ in. (220 × 161 mm.); spine: vertical, in gold, '*Geography III* / *Elizabeth Bishop Farrar, Straus & Giroux*'.

Dust Jacket, by Cynthia Krupat: front: 'within double deep Blue (179) border on l. yellowish Brown (76.5 close, no exact Centroid equivalent) paper, in Black (267), *Geography III* / *Elizabeth Bishop* | [in Black, within deep B border: etching identical to the one on the cover page'; spine: vertical, in Black, '*Geography III* / *Elizabeth Bishop Farrar, Straus and Giroux*'; back: within double deep B border, in Black, '*By Elizabeth*

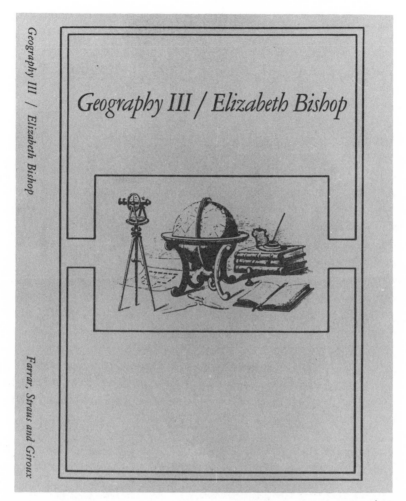

A13

Bishop | [rule] | *North & South* | *A Cold Spring* | *Questions of Travel* | *The Complete Poems* | *The Diary of "Helena Morley"* (*translator*) | *Contemporary Brazilian Poetry* (*co-editor*) | [rule] | *Farrar, Straus and Giroux*' front flap: '[double deep B rule] | [in Black] $7.95 || John Ashbery, in sponsoring Elizabeth | Bishop for the 1976 *Books Abroad* / Neu-|stadt International Prize for Literature, | wrote: "The extraordinary thing about | Miss Bishop is that she is both a public | and a private poet, or perhaps it is that | her poetry by its very existence renders | obsolete these two after all artificial dis-|tinctions (artificial insofar as poetry is | concerned). The private self—the quirk-|iness, the rightness of vision, the special | sights and events (a moose, a filling sta-|tion) that have intrigued Miss Bishop to | the point of poetry —melts imperceptibly | into the larger utterance, the grandeur of | poetry, which, because it remains rooted | in everyday particulars, never sounds | 'grand,' but is as quietly convincing as | honest speech." | [¶] These words apply perfectly to Miss | Bishop's new book, *Geography III*. | Among other recent poems, it contains | "The Moose," "Crusoe in England," | "Poem," "In the Waiting Room," "The | End of March," "Night City," "Five | Flights Up," the prose poem "12 O'Clock || *(continued on back flap)* || [double deep B rule]'; back flap: '[double deep B rule]'; '*(continued from front flap)* || News," the villanelle "One Art," and | "Objects & Apparitions," translated from | the Spanish of Octavio Paz. | [¶] As Marie-Claire Blais, Miss Bishop's | second sponsor for this award, pointed | out: "The body of her work is relatively | small, but one cannot read a single | line either of her poetry or prose without | feeling that a real poet is speaking . . . | whose eye is both an inner and outer eye. | The outer eye sees with marvelous, ob-|jective precision and the vision is trans-|lated into quite simple language." | [¶] *Geography III* is Miss Bishop's fifth | book of poetry, following *North & South* | (1946), *A Cold Spring* (1955), *Ques-|tions of Travel* (1965), and *The Com-|plete Poems* (1969). || *Jacket design by Cynthia Krupat* || *Farrar, Straus and Giroux* | *19 Union Square West* | *New York 10003* || ISBN 0–374–16135–6 | [double deep B rule]'.

Text Contents: "From 'First Lesson in Geography,' Monteith's Geographical Series, A.S. Barnes & Co., 1884," "In the Waiting Room," "Crusoe in England," "Night City," "The Moose (for Grace Bulmer Bowers)," "12 O'Clock News," "Poem," "One Art," "End of March (for John Malcolm Brinnin and Bill Read: Duxbury)," tr. of Octavio Paz's "Objects and Apparitions (for Joseph Cornell)," "Five Flights Up."

Publication: first printing: 7,500 copies on December 28, 1976.

Locations: CWM, DLC (deposit copy stamped 22 December 1976), EB, MoSW (with dust jacket), TxR, TxU.

A13.[a2]   *Geography III.* Second printing, 1978 (first edition, third impression, paperback, Smyth sewn)

Geography III / Elizabeth Bishop | [etching] | FARRAR, STRAUS AND GIROUX / NEW YORK

Same as **A13** except:

Paper and Binding: leaf and paper wrapper measure 8⁷⁄₁₆ × 6 in. (215 × 153 mm.); yWhite (Centroid 92) wove paper; all edges trimmed; stiff glazed l. yellowish Brown (76) paper wrapper printed in a design similar to the dust jacket of **A13**; front wrapper: '[within a double d. greenish Blue (174) border, in Black 267)] *Geography III / Elizabeth Bishop* | [black etching within a double d.gB border]'; spine: in Black '*Geography III / Elizabeth Bishop   Farrar, Straus and Giroux*'; back wrapper: in Black within a double d.gB border, 'N579 $3.95 | ISBN 0–374–51440–2 | *Elizabeth Bishop* | *GEOGRAPHY III* | *Winner of the Poetry Award of the National Book Critics' Circle* || John Ashbery, in sponsoring Elizabeth Bishop for the 1976 | *Books Abroad /* Neustadt Prize for Literature: || "The extraordinary thing about Miss Bishop is that she is both | a public and a private poet, or perhaps it is that her poetry by | its very existence renders obsolete these two after all artificial distinctions (artificial insofar as poetry is concerned). The | private self—the quirkiness, the rightness of vision, the special | sights and events (a moose, a filling station) that have in-|trigued Miss Bishop to the point of poetry—melts imperceptibly | into the larger utterance,

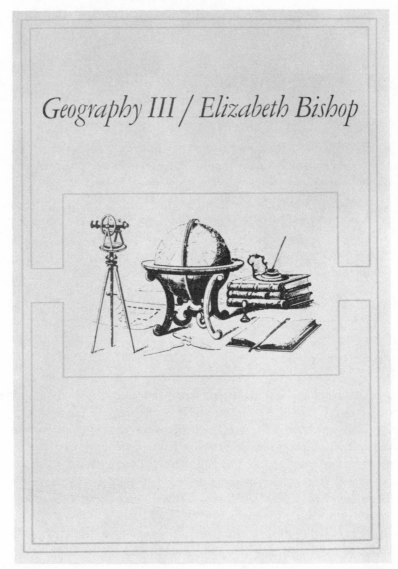

Geography III / Elizabeth Bishop

A13.[a2]

the grandeur of poetry, which, be-|cause it remains rooted in everyday particulars, never sounds | 'grand', but is as quietly convincing as honest speech." || Marie-Claire Blais, Miss Bishop's second sponsor: || "The body of her work is relatively small, but one cannot read | a single line either of her poetry or prose without feeling that | a real poet is speaking . . . whose eye is both an inner and outer | eye. The outer eye sees with marvelous objective precision and | the vision is translated into quite simple language." || Herbert Leibowitz, in *The New York Times Book Review:* || "For over forty years, Elizabeth Bishop's immaculately wrought | poems have earned her the reputation of the poet's poet. With | its calmly circumspect being and elegant finish, deploying | space in formally perfect patterns, each small portfolio of work | resembles classical architecture." || *Cover design by Cynthia Krupat* || Farrar, Straus and Giroux | 19 Union Square West | New York 10003'.

Publication: 5,070 copies in 1978, at $3.95.

A13.[b1] *Geography III.* Chatto and Windus, London, 1977 (first edition, second impression, paperback, produced by offset, Smyth sewn)

Title Page: 8⅜ × 5⅜ in. (215 × 138 mm.).

Published by
Chatto and Windus Ltd, 40 William IV Street, London WC2

All rights reserved. No part of this publication may be reproduced, stored in
a retrieval system, or transmitted, in any form, or by any means, electronic,
mechanical, photocopying, recording or otherwise, without the prior permission
of Chatto & Windus Ltd.

All the poems in this book originally appeared in *The New Yorker*. Elizabeth
Bishop's translation of "Objects & Apparitions" by Octavio Paz copyright
©1974 by The New Yorker Magazine, Inc.

Designed by Cynthia Krupat

        British Library Cataloguing in Publication Data
            Bishop, Elizabeth
              Geography III.
              I. Title
              811'.5'2   PS3503.I785
              ISBN 0-7011-2238-2

Copyright ©1971, 1972, 1973, 1974, 1975, 1976
by Elizabeth Bishop

Printed in Great Britain by
Redwood Burn Limited
Trowbridge & Esher.

Same as **A**13 except:

Paper and Binding: leaf and paper wrapper measure 8⅜ × 5⅜ in. (215
× 138 mm.); yWhite (Centroid 92) wove paper; all edges trimmed;
stiff, glazed White (263) paper wrapper printed in d. Blue (183) and
v.deep Red (14); front wrapper: '[in d.B] *Geography III* | [in v.deep R
rule] | *Elizabeth Bishop* | [d.B etching from title page extending to
spine and back]'; spine: '[in d.B] *ELIZABETH BISHOP* [in v.deep R]
GEOGRAPHY III [part of d.B drawing] C & W'; back wrapper: in
d.B | In sponsoring Elizabeth Bishop for the 1976 | *Books Abroad/*
Neustadt International Prize for | Poetry, John Ashbery said: "The
private self— | the quirkiness, the rightness of vision, the | special
sights and events that have intrigued | Miss Bishop to the point of
poetry—melts | imperceptibly into the larger utterance, the | grandeur
of poetry, which, because it remains | rooted in everyday particulars,
never sounds | 'grand', but is as quietly convincing as honest speech."
| [¶] These words apply perfectly to Elizabeth | Bishop's new book,
Geography III. The poems | here range in place from Crusoe's island
with its | "fifty-two miserable, small volcanoes" to an | encounter with
a moose in the New Brunswick | woods, and include a strange expe-
rience | incurred while reading the *National Geographic* | in a dentist's
waiting-room and a thought-|provoking, perhaps fear-inspiring inter-

Geography III

Elizabeth Bishop

A13.[b1]

preta-|tion of the geography and demography of a | writing desk. ||
"An extraordinary meticulousness of crafts-|manship marks all her
work; exactitude of | perception plays against inherently nostalgic or |
romantically tragic themes, to give great subtlety and toughness."
Malcolm Bradbury || "Miss Bishop is a very old admiration; I think | no
one is writing as many good poems in | English." *Robert Lowell* | [¶]
Geography III is Elizabeth Bishop's fifth book | of poetry, following
North & South, Questions of | *Travel* and the *Complete Poems* of 1970. It
won | the 1976 Poetry Award of the National Book | Critics Circle of
America. || [flush right] | *2.50 net* | ISBN 0 7011 2238 2 | [flush
right] *in U.K. Only'.*

Publication: first printing: 1,000 copies on August 25, 1977, at 2.5 net.

Locations: CWM, DLC, EB.

A14 *One Art.* [The International Poetry Forum, Pittsburgh, 1978] (first edition, first impression)

ONE ART

[facsimile of the poem "One Art" in Elizabeth Bishop's handwriting, signed Elizabeth Bishop]

Broadside: 11 × 8½ in. (279 × 215 mm.).

Collation: broadside.

Contents: recto: "One Art"; an incorrect acknowledgment: "From *The Complete Poems* by Elizabeth Bishop . . .".

Paper and Typography: 11 × 8½ in. (279 × 215 mm.); unglazed, yWhite (Centroid 92) wove paper; top and fore edges trimmed, bottom edge rough trimmed and stained d. reddish Gray (23). The poem is in EB's own hand. The acknowledgment is typed.

Publication: 350 copies distributed at EB's reading for The International Poetry Forum, February 1, 1978, inside *The International Poetry Forum Presents Elizabeth Bishop.*

A15 *One Art.* Friends of the Smith College Library, Northampton, Massachusetts, 1979 (second edition, first impression)

ONE ART *by Elizabeth Bishop*

The art of losing isn't hard to master;
so many things seem filled with the intent
to be lost that their loss is no disaster.

Lose something every day. Accept the fluster
of lost door keys, the hour badly spent.
The art of losing isn't hard to master.

Then practice losing farther, losing faster:
places, and names, and where it was you meant
to travel. None of these will bring disaster.

I lost my mother's watch. And look! my last, or
next-to-last, of three loved houses went.
The art of losing isn't hard to master.

I lost two cities, lovely ones. And, vaster,
some realms I owned, two rivers, a continent.
I miss them, but it wasn't a disaster.

—Even losing you (the joking voice, a gesture
I love) I shan't have lied. It's evident
the art of losing's not too hard to master
though it may look like (*Write* it!) like disaster.

200 copies of this keepsake were printed at the Catawba Press
on the occasion of a lecture by Susan Van Dyne for
the Friends of the Smith College Library, 31 March 1979.

"One Art" from *Geography III* by Elizabeth Bishop. Copyright © 1976 by Elizabeth
Bishop. Reprinted with the permission of Farrar, Straus & Giroux, Inc.
This poem appeared originally in *The New Yorker*.

Broadside: 11½ × 6⅟₁₆ in. (293 × 155 mm.).

Collation: broadside.

Contents: "One Art," colophon.

Paper and Typography: 11½ × 6¹⁄₁₆ in. (293 × 155 mm.); unglazed yWhite (Centroid 92) wove paper; all edges trimmed; text: 18/21 Bembo roman.

Colophon: '*200 copies of this keepsake were printed at the Catawba Press | on the occasion of a lecture by Susan Van Dyne for | the Friends of the Smith College Library, 31 March 1979.* || "One Art" from *Geography III* by Elizabeth Bishop. Copyright © 1976 by Elizabeth | Bishop. Reprinted by permission of Farrar, Straus & Giroux, Inc. | This poem appeared originally in *The New Yorker*.'

Publication: 200 copies on March 31, 1979. Miss Bishop was not present; however, a significant portion of Ms. Van Dyne's lecture concerned EB's work.

A16 *North Haven*. Lord John Press, Northridge, Calif., 1979 (first edition, first impression)

Broadside: 20¾ × 14½ in. (520 × 352 mm.).

Collation: broadside.

Contents: drawing of North Haven by Kit Barker; "North Haven"; colophon.

Paper and Typography: 20¾ × 14½ in. (520 × 352 mm.); unglazed yWhite (Centroid 92) wove paper, Arches Cover Stock; top and fore edges trimmed, bottom edge rough trimmed; title: 30 pt. Centaur caps, text: 18/19 Centaur roman and Arrighi italic printed in Black (267); drawing printed in m. Blue (182) and d. Blue (183).

Colophon: 'Designed and printed by Richard Bigus for the Lord John Press. Illustrated by Kit Barker. | Copyright © 1979 by Elizabeth Bishop. Limited to 150 signed copies. | This is number'. Copy numbers written beneath in pencil.

Publication: 150 copies signed on September 26, 1979. In addition to the 150 copies, there were 25 presentation copies, a number of which remain unsigned, and 6 signed copies that were printed with the name of the recipient: the author, the printer, the publisher, the artist, Ilse Barker, and Candace W. MacMahon.

NORTH HAVEN

IN MEMORIAM: ROBERT LOWELL

I can make out the rigging of a schooner
a mile off; I can count
the new cones on the spruce. It is so still
the pale bay wears a milky skin, the sky
no clouds, except for one long, carded, horse's-tail.

The islands haven't shifted since last summer,
even if I like to pretend they have
—drifting, in a dreamy sort of way,
a little north, a little south or sidewise,
and that they're free within the blue frontiers of bay.

This month, our favorite one is full of flowers:
Buttercups, Red Clover, Purple Vetch,
Hawkweed still burning, Daisies pied, Eyebright,
the Fragrant Bedstraw's incandescent stars,
and more, returned, to paint the meadows with delight.

The Goldfinches are back, or others like them,
and the White-throated Sparrow's five-note song,
pleading and pleading, brings tears to the eyes.
Nature repeats herself, or almost does:
repeat, repeat, repeat; revise, revise, revise.

Years ago, you told me it was here
(in 1932?) you first "discovered *girls*"
and learned to sail, and learned to kiss.
You had "such fun", you said, that classic summer.
("Fun"—it always seemed to leave you at a loss...)

You left North Haven, anchored in its rock,
afloat in mystic blue...And now—you've left
for good. You can't derange, or re-arrange,
your poems again. (But the Sparrows can their song.)
The words won't change again. Sad friend, you cannot change.

ELIZABETH BISHOP

Designed and printed by Richard Bigus for the Lord John Press. Illustrated by Kit Barker.
Copyright © 1979 by Elizabeth Bishop. Limited to 250 signed copies.
This is number

B

Contributions to Books

B1   *Vassarion, 1934* (Yearbook edited by EB).

[pink] THE | NINETEEN THIRTY FOUR | [black] VASSAR-ION | [Vassar College Seal] | VOLUME 45 | *Published by the* | [pink] SENIOR CLASS | [black] *Vassar College, Poughkeepsie, New York*

[1–20] 21–30 [31–33] 34–87 [88–89] 90–95 [96–100] 101–104 [105–106] 107–126 [127–128] 129–155 [156–148]. 10¾ × 8 in. Maroon velvet cover. Impressed on front: 'VASSARION'. Pink endpapers. All edges trimmed.

Contains EB's photograph three times: Senior Year, p. 48; *Vassar Miscellany News*, p. 101 (front row, first on the left); *Vassarion*, p. 103 (front row, center).

B2   *Trial Balances* (1935)

[double rule] | [rule] | *TRIAL BALANCES* | *Edited by* | Ann Winslow | NEW YORK | THE MACMILLAN COMPANY | 1935 | [rule] | [double rule]

[i–iv] v–vii [viii] ix–xi [xii] xiii–xvi [xvii–xviii], 1–217 [218] 219–225 [226–230]. 8¾ × 5⅞ in. Dark blue cloth stamped in silver, front and spine. White endpapers. Top and bottom edges trimmed; fore edge rough trimmed. Silver dust jacket printed in blue.

Contains "The Reprimand," "The Map," and "Three Valentines," with a commentary by Marianne Moore, pp. 78–83.

Note: this is the first book appearance for EB as a poet.

Publication: 2,500 copies on October 8, 1935, at $2.00. The plates were destroyed on March 10, 1936, and the rights were returned in April 1952.

First Appearance:
"The Reprimand"   Not reprinted
"The Map"   NS, Po, CP / P, S
   first letter of the first word in each line capitalized]   ~ *not capitalized*
   NS+
   12   blossom‸]   ~, NS+   14   sea-shore]   seashore NS+
"Three Valentines"   Not reprinted
   Note: I and II are reprinted unchanged from the *Vassar Review* (C37, C38). III appears only in this volume.

B3   *New Directions in Prose and Poetry (1936)*

NEW DIRECTIONS | in | Prose and Poetry | [rule] | Edited by | James Laughlin IV | NEW DIRECTIONS | NORFOLK, CT. | 1936

104 leaves; unpaged. 9¼ × 6¼ in. Yellow paper-covered boards printed in red and black on front; in black on spine. Yellowish white endpapers. All edges trimmed. No dust jacket.

Paper Issue: 8¹⁵/₁₆ × 6 in. Similar in color and design to the hardbound.

Contains "Casabianca," "The Gentleman of Shalot," and "The Colder the Air," pp. 82–84 (**C45, C46, C47**).

Publication: about 700 hardbound copies, at $2.00, and 507 copies in paper, at $2.00, on November 16, 1936. 234 hardbound and 100 paper copies went to New Books, London.

Note: According to J. M. Edelstein (*Wallace Stevens: A Bibliography*, University of Pittsburgh, 1973, p. 159) the hardcover volumes were sold at $2.00; he lists no price for the paperback. According to Robert A. Wilson (*Gertrude Stein: A Bibliography*, Phoenix Book Shop, 1973, p. 94) publisher's records show only that the paperback sold for $2.00; there is no record of the hardcover price. *New Directions in Prose and*

Poetry (1937) contains an ad for available copies of the 1936 volume at $2.00 but does not mention whether copies were paperback or hardcover.

B4   *New Letters in America* (1937)

NEW LETTERS | IN AMERICA | EDITOR | HORACE GREGORY | ASSOCIATE EDITOR | ELEANOR CLARK | W · W · NORTON & COMPANY | PUBLISHERS · NEW YORK

[1–6] 7–16 [17–18] 19–222 [223–224]. 8¾ × 5¾ in. Off-white cloth cover stamped in red and black on front and spine. Yellowish white endpapers. All edges trimmed; top edge stained red. Red and white dust jacket printed in black and white.

Contains "The Sea and Its Shore," pp. 19–25 (**C55**).

Publication: 800–900 copies on September 9, 1937, at $2.00.

B5   *New Directions in Prose and Poetry* (1939)

NEW DIRECTIONS | IN PROSE & POETRY | 1939 | [publisher's device] | NEW DIRECTIONS · NORFOLK · CONN.

[i–vi] vii–xi [xii] xiii–xxii [xxiii–xxiv], [1–2] 3–174, four leaves of photographs, 175–189 [190], six leaves of photographs, 191–390, eighteen leaves of advertising. 8 × 5⅝ in. All edges trimmed. Bound in unglazed white paper over boards printed in medium blue and bright red, on front; blue printed in white on spine; solid white, on back. White endpapers. Dust jacket front and spine, white printed in red and blue; back, white printed in blue.

Contains "The Monument," pp. 76–78.

Publication: 1,000 copies on November 1, 1939, at $2.50.

First Appearance:
"The Monument"   NS, Po, CP / S

first letter of the first word in each line capitalized] ~*not capitalized*
NS+
50 The] —The NS+   68 Its] The NS+

B6 *New Poems: 1940* (1941)

[six rules] | NEW POEMS: | 1940 | An Anthology of British and
American Verse | Edited by Oscar Williams [ornament] A Living
Age Book | The Yardstick Press [ornament] New York [ornament]
1941 | [six rules]

[i–ii], [1–8] 9–13 [14] 15–18 [19–20] 21–261 [262–270] 271 [272]
273–276 [277–278]; pp. [263–270]: photographs of the poets; p. [265]:
photograph of Elizabeth Bishop in a broad-brimmed straw hat. 8¼ ×
5⅜ in. Neutral cloth cover stamped in red and gold on spine. White
endpapers. Top edges trimmed and stained red; fore and bottom edges
rough trimmed. Red dust jacket printed in black and white with the
names of the contributors.

Contains "Roosters," pp. 69–74 (**C68**).

Publication: issued on April 17, 1941, at $2.50.

B7 *American Decade* (1943)

AMERICAN DECADE | 68 Poems for the First Time in an An-
thology | *by* ELIZABETH BISHOP, R. P. BLACKMUR, TOM
BOGGS, | MYRON H. BROOMELL, JOHN CIARDI, ROBERT
CLAIRMONT, | MALCOLM COWLEY, E. E. CUMMINGS,
REUEL DENNEY, | THOMAS W. DUNCAN, KENNETH
FEARING, THOMAS HORNSBY | FERRIL, LLOYD FRAN-
KENBERG, ROBERT FROST, CLIFFORD | GESSLER, W. W.
GIBSON, HORACE GREGORY, LANGSTON | HUGHES,
ROBINSON JEFFERS, WELDON KEES, E. L. MAYO, | JO-
SEPHINE MILES, SAMUEL FRENCH MORSE, MURIEL |
RUKEYSER, CARL SANDBURG, WINFIELD TOWNLEY
SCOTT, | KARL JAY SHAPIRO, THEODORE SPENCER,
WALLACE | STEVENS, MARK VAN DOREN, EDWARD
WEISMILLER, | JOHN WHEELWRIGHT, WILLIAM CAR-
LOS WILLIAMS | [ornament] | *EDITED BY TOM BOGGS* |

And star-dials pointed to morn.—POE | [ornament] | THE CUM-MINGTON PRESS, *Publishers*

[1–10] 11–93 [94–96]. 9¹¹⁄₁₆ × 6⁵⁄₁₆ in. Blue cloth cover stamped in white on spine. Yellowish white endpapers. Top edge trimmed; fore and bottom edges rough trimmed. White dust jacket printed in blue.

Contains "Song: Letter to New York," p. 11, and "The Weed," pp. 12–13 (**C67, C48**).

Colophon: p. [96]: 'AMERICAN DECADE | has been set up in Linotype Baskerville and printed | by The Southworth-Anthoensen Press at Portland, | Maine. Four hundred seventy-five copies, of which | fifty are not for sale, are on Andria paper, and twenty-|five, especially bound by hand and numbered 1 to | 25, on Sterling Laid. It has been designed and | published by The Cummington Press | Cummington, Massachusetts. | [ornament]'.

Publication: 475 copies, at $3.50, and 25 handbound copies, at $7.50, on June 24, 1943. The binding for the 25 copies consists of blue, white, and black paper-covered boards with natural-colored linen back and white paper label printed downward on spine.

B8 *New Voices Atlantic Anthology* (1945)

NEW VOICES | [double rule] | ATLANTIC | ANTHOLOGY | EDITED | BY | NICHOLAS MOORE | *and* | DOUGLAS NEWTON | THE FORTUNE PRESS | LONDON, S.W.1

[i–vi] vii–x [xi–xii], 1–202 [203–204]; eight unnumbered photographs are not reflected in the pagination formula, one following each of pages 26, 36, 60, 98, 120, 140, 176, 198. 9 × 6 in. Reddish brown cloth stamped in gold on spine. Yellowish white endpapers. Top edges trimmed; fore and bottom edges rough trimmed.

Contains a reprinting of "The Weed," pp. 90–91, and "Roosters," pp. 91–95, and the first book appearance of "The Imaginary Iceberg," pp. 95–96 (**C48, C68, C43**). This is the first book appearance for EB in England.

Publication: issued in 1945.

B9   *A Little Treasury of Modern Poetry* (1946)

[all within an orange inset printed in white and black] *A* | *Little Treasury* | *of* | *Modern Poetry* | ENGLISH & AMERICAN | *Edited with an Introduction by* | *Oscar Williams* | [device] | NEW YORK | CHARLES SCRIBNER'S SONS | 1946

[1–6] 7–44 [45–46] 47–622 [623–624], eight leaves of photographs of poets, but not of EB, 641–672. 6⁷⁄₁₆ × 4¼ in. Dark blue cloth on front, light blue cloth stamped in red and gold on spine. Yellowish white endpapers. All edges trimmed; top edges gilded. Blue and white dust jacket printed in black, yellow, and white.

Contains a reprinting of "Roosters," p. 67, and the first American book appearance of "The Imaginary Iceberg," p. 422 (**C68, C43**).

Publication: 10,000 copies on June 24, 1946, at $2.75.

B10   *The Partisan Reader* (1946)

[vertical] THE | PARTISAN | [vertical] READER | TEN YEARS OF PARTISAN REVIEW | 1934–1944: AN ANTHOLOGY | EDITED BY | WILLIAM PHILLIPS AND PHILIP RAHV | INTRODUCTION BY | LIONEL TRILLING | THE DIAL PRESS, NEW YORK, 1946

[i–iv] [v–xvi], [1–2] 3–212 [213–214] 215–285 [286–287] 288–581 [582–584] 585–677 [678] 679–688. 8⅜ × 5⅝ in. Yellow cloth stamped in black, front and spine. White endpapers. All edges trimmed. Gray and white dust jacket printed in yellow, white, and red.

Contains "Love Lies Sleeping," pp. 221–222, which appeared in *North & South*, and "In Prison," pp. 20–27, its first book appearance (**C56, C57**).

Publication: issued on September 9, 1946, at $3.75.

B11   *The Best American Short Stories* (1949)

THE | *Best* | AMERICAN | SHORT STORIES | 1949 | [ornamental rule] | *and The Yearbook of the American Short Story* | [rule] | *Edited by* MARTHA FOLEY | 19[publisher's device]49 | [rule] | HOUGHTON MIFFLIN COMPANY BOSTON | The Riverside Press Cambridge

[i–vi] vii–xvi [xvii–xviii], 1–334. 8⅜ × 5½ in. Light green cloth cover stamped in green, front and spine. Yellowish white endpapers. All edges trimmed.

Contains "The Farmer's Children," pp. 39–47 (**C81**).

Publication: 9,000 copies on July 12, 1949, at $3.50.

B12 *Mid-Century American Poets* (1950)

[all within a double rule border 6⅞ × 3¾ in.] EDITED *by* JOHN CIARDI | Mid-Century | American | Poets | [device] | [rule] | *Twayne Publishers, Inc. New York 4*

[i–viii] ix–xxx [xxxi–xxxvi], 1–300. 8⅜ × 5½ in. Deep aqua cloth stamped in light blue, front and spine. White endpapers. All edges trimmed. Buff dust jacket printed in blue and yellow.

Contains an uncollected essay, "It All Depends," as well as poems already printed in *North & South*: "The Colder the Air," "Large Bad Picture," "The Man-Moth," "Sleeping on the Ceiling," "A Miracle for Breakfast," "Cirque d'Hiver," "Jerónimo's House," "The Fish," "Songs for a Colored Singer," pp. 267–280 (**C46, C76, C44, C61, C51, C65, C69, C66, C72**).

Publication: 2,000 copies in 1950, at $4.00.

B13 *Poetry Awards 1952* (1952)

[two ornamental rules, left; two ornamental rules, right] | *Poetry Awards* | 1952 | [two ornamental rules, centered] A COMPILA-TION OF ORIGINAL POETRY | PUBLISHED IN MAGA-ZINES OF THE | ENGLISH SPEAKING WORLD | IN 1951 | [publisher's device] | PHILADELPHIA | UNIVERSITY OF PENNSYLVANIA PRESS | 1952 [i–iv] v–vii [viii] ix–xii [xiii–xiv], 1–54 [55–56] 57–62 [63–64]. 8¾ × 5⁹⁄₁₆ in. Burgundy cloth stamped in white on spine. White endpapers. All edges trimmed. Pink dust jacket printed in red.

Contains "The Prodigal," p. 9 (**C97**).

Publication: 1,500 copies in December 1952, at $2.50.

B14   *The New Partisan Reader* (1953)

[device] | THE NEW PARTISAN READER | 1945–1953 | EDITED BY | *William Phillips* | AND | *Philip Rahv* | HARCOURT, BRACE AND COMPANY [device] NEW YORK

[i–xii], [1]–[626], numbered irregularly. 8⅜ × 5⅝ in. Light blue cloth stamped in black, front and spine. White endpapers. All edges trimmed. Dust jacket front and spine printed in green, maize, and white; back, white printed in green.

Contains a reprinting of "Anaphora" as well as the first book appearance of "Over 2000 Illustrations and a Complete Concordance," pp. 151–153 (**C73, C84**).

Publication: 4,375 copies on October 22, 1953, at $6.75.

B15   *Modern Architecture in Brazil* (1956)

Henrique E. Mindlin | MODERN | ARCHITECTURE | IN BRAZIL | PREFACE BY PROF. S. GIEDION | [device] | REINHOLD PUBLISHING CORPORATION | NEW YORK

[I–VIII] IX–XIII [XIV], 1–256. 11¾ × 8½ in. Yellow cloth cover stamped in gold, front and spine. White endpapers. All edges trimmed.

Contains an acknowledgment to EB "who put into shape the Portuguese original for the introductory text and for the first comments on individual examples," p. xiii.

B16   *New Poems* (1957)

NEW | POEMS | BY AMERICAN POETS | No. 2 | *edited by* *Rolfe Humphries* | Ballantine Books · New York · 1957 | [rule]

[i–xii] 1–179 [180]. 7¼ × 5⅜ in. Buff cloth cover stamped in red on spine. Buff, red, and white dust wrapper printed in black and white.

Contains the only reprinting of "The Wit," p. 23, and the first reprinting of "Squatter's Children," p. 22 (C110, C112).

Publication: issued August 15, 1957, at $3.00.

Paper Issue:

NEW | POEMS | BY AMERICAN POETS | #2 | *edited by* *Rolfe Humphries* | Ballantine Books · New York · 1957

7¹³⁄₁₆ × 4 in. Stiff, glazed red, blue, and white paper wrapper printed in black, red, white, and blue. All edges trimmed. Contents same as the hardcover.

Publication: issued August 15, 1957, at $3.00.

B17   *Best Poems of 1957* (1958)

BEST POEMS | of 1957 | BORESTONE MOUNTAIN | POETRY AWARDS | 1958 | *A Compilation of Original Poetry* | *published in* | *Magazines of the English-speaking World* | *in 1957* | *Tenth Annual Issue* | [publisher's device] | STANFORD UNIVERSITY PRESS · STANFORD, CALIFORNIA | 1958

[i–x], [1–3] 4–99 [100–102]. 8¾ × 5⅝ in. Neutral cloth cover stamped in gray on spine. Yellowish white endpapers. All edges trimmed. Purple dust jacket, mauve on spine, printed in lavender and white with the names of the contributors.

Contains "The Armadillo—Brazil," pp. 17–18 (C117).

Publication: 1,500 copies in December 1958, at $2.95.

Note: this volume contains an erratum sheet concerning E. E. Cummings's poem which should have been listed in the Table of Contents under "Poems Not Entered in Contest."

B18   *Stories from* The New Yorker (1960)

STORIES FROM | THE | NEW YORKER | 1950–1960 |
19[device]60 | SIMON AND SCHUSTER · NEW YORK

[i–iv] v–vii [viii–xiii], 1–780 [781–786(three blank leaves)]. 9⁵⁄₁₆ × 6¼
in. Gray blue cloth stamped in black on front and black and gold on
spine. Yellowish white endpapers. All edges trimmed.

Contains "In the Village," pp. 290–308 (**C105**).

Publication: issued in 1960, at $7.50.

B19   *Best Poems of 1960* (1962)

BEST POEMS | of 1960 | BORESTONE MOUNTAIN |
POETRY AWARDS | 1961 | *A Compilation of Original Poetry* |
published in | *Magazines of the English-speaking World in 1960* |
THIRTEENTH ANNUAL ISSUE | VOLUME XIII | PACIFIC
BOOKS, PUBLISHERS · PALO ALTO, CALIFORNIA | 1962

[i–xii], [1–3] 4–124. 8¾ × 5⅝ in. Neutral cloth cover stamped in black
on spine. White endpapers. All edges trimmed. Black dust jacket
printed in gray and white with the names of the contributors.

Contains "Song for a Rainy Season," pp. 15–16 (**C124**).

Publication: 1,000 hardbound copies at $3.50 and 500 paper copies at
$1.50 in December 1961.

Note: I have not seen a paper copy.

B20   *Poet's Choice* (1962)

POET'S | CHOICE | [ornamental rule] | EDITED BY | Paul
Engle and Joseph Langland | [publisher's device] | THE DIAL
PRESS NEW YORK 1962

[i–iv] v–vii [viii] ix–xi [xii] xiii–xvii [xviii–xx], 1–291 [292] 293–303
[304–306]. 9⁵⁄₁₆ × 6¼ in. Deep red cloth stamped in gold on spine.

Orange endpapers. Top edges trimmed; fore and bottom edges rough trimmed. Cream dust jacket printed in orange, gold, and black.

Contains a reprinting of "The Man-Moth," with an original commentary printed for the first time, pp. 103–105 (C44).

Publication: issued on October 9, 1962, at $6.00 until December 31, 1962, thereafter at $6.75.

Paper Issue: 5¹⁄₇ × 8 in. Wrapper having the same design as dust jacket. Same contents.

Publication: 2,345 copies on April 22, 1963, at $1.45.

B21   *The Partisan Review Anthology* (1962)

[Two pages: left] The Partisan [right] Review Anthology | [rule] | Edited by William Phillips and Philip Rahv | [left: rule; right] HOLT, RINEHART AND WINSTON · NEW YORK

[i–vi] vii [viii–x], [1–2] 3–279 [280–282] 283–359 [360–362] 363–391 [392–394] 395–490. 9⁷⁄₁₆ × 6¼ in. Off-white cloth on front and back, gray cloth stamped in gold on spine. White endpapers with blue silk threads. Brown dust jacket printed in white and red with the names of the contributors.

Contains "Visits to St. Elizabeths," pp. 381–382 (C116).

Publication: issued in 1962, at $8.50.

B22   *Best Poems of 1962* (1963)

BEST POEMS | of 1962 | BORESTONE MOUNTAIN | POETRY AWARDS | 1963 | *A Compilation of Original Poetry* | *published in* | *Magazines of the English-speaking World* | *in 1962* | FIFTEENTH ANNUAL ISSUE | VOLUME XV | PACIFIC BOOKS, PUBLISHERS · PALO ALTO, CALIFORNIA | 1963

[i–xiv], [1–3] 4–160 [161–162]. 8¹³⁄₁₆ × 5⅝ in. Neutral cloth cover stamped in purple on spine. White endpapers. All edges trimmed.

Paper Issue: 8½ × 5½ in. Stiff, glazed paper wrapper. Lavender, on front, printed in purple and white; white, on spine, printed in purple; white back. All edges trimmed.

Contains "Sandpiper," p. 19 (**C129**).

Publication: 1,000 hardbound copies at $3.50 and 432 copies at $1.50 in November 1963.

B23   *Randall Jarrell* (1967)

Randall Jarrell | [rule] | 1914–1965 | EDITED BY | Robert Lowell, Peter Taylor, | & Robert Penn Warren | [publisher's device] | *Farrar, Straus & Giroux* | NEW YORK

[i–vi] vii–xii, [1, 2] 3–301 [302–304] 305–307 [308]. 8¼ × 5⅝ in. Gray reddish brown cloth cover impressed on front and stamped in gold on spine. Bright yellow endpapers. All edges trimmed, top edges stained green. Black and yellow dust jacket, printed in yellow, black, and white.

Contains "An Inadequate Tribute," pp. 20–21.

Publication: issued in 1967 at $6.50.

B24   *Woodlawn North* (1970)

Woodlawn North | A BOOK OF POEMS | by Milton Kessler | *ETCHINGS by ROBERT MARX* | WITH A PREFACE BY ELI-ZABETH BISHOP | IMPRESSIONS WORKSHOP

32 leaves; unpaged. 11¾ × 8¾ in. Natural linen cloth cover. Yellow-ish white endpapers. All edges trimmed. No dust jacket.

Contains "Preface" by EB, p. [9]: '[¶] Dear reader, *Woodlawn North* is a small | collection of very sad poems. Mr. Kessler goes | rapidly—descends might be a better word—from | lyrics about shells, bells, songs and roses, to | themes of childhood misfortune, family trib-|ulation, death, loss and mourning. But even | in the saddest poems the voice of a lyric | poet rises and re-asserts itself, and the songs | and bells keep re-appearing. In the narrow | space of this collection Mr. Kessler shows

| himself to be a poet of deep, real, family sen-|timent and a lyricist capable of lovely and | musical effects. (See "A Bombardi :r's Land-| scape", or the first stanza of part two of "Sum-|mer's Enc", my own favorite.) | *Elizabeth Bishop*'.

Colophon: p. [61]: '*WOODLAWN NORTH* has been printed in an edition | of 125 copies, numbered 1 through 125. The print-|ing was completed on April 14, 1970, at Impressions | Workshop in Boston, and all copies have been signed | by the poet & the artist. The etchings were executed | and printed by Robert Marx. The book was designed, | handset in Garamond, & printed on Velke Losiny | (a Czechoslovak handmade paper) by | Michael McCurdy. The book was | handbound in cloth by | Ivan Ruzicka. | [ornament] | *Grateful | acknowledgement is made to | the following periodicals, where some | of these poems first appeared: Chelsea Review, | Choice, Epoch, Lace Curtain, The Na-|tion, and The Transatlantic | Review.* | [ornament] | This is copy number | [rule] | [signature of author] | [signature of illustrator]'.

Publication: 125 copies in 1970, at $45.00.

Note: an abstract from this preface was reprinted as a dust jacket comment on Kessler's *Sailing Too Far*, Harper and Row, 1973: ' "Even in the saddest poems the voice of a lyric poet rises and reasserts itself, | and the songs and bells keep reappearing. . . . A lyricist capable of lovely | and musical effects." | —ELIZABETH BISHOP'.

B25 *A Second Talent* (1971)

[self-wrapper] A SECOND TALENT | [vertical rule] | An exhibition of | drawings | and paintings | by writers | [drawing] | *9 Mr. Max Beerbohm receives an Influential tho Biased, Disputation . . . by Max Beerbohm* | [on back] THE ARTS CLUB OF CHICAGO | [drawing] | *175 untitled drawing by William Makepiece Thackeray* | November 15 through December 31, 1971 | 109 East Ontario Street, Chicago

24 leaves; unpaged. 10 × 8 in. Stiff, unglazed, brown paper wrapper, printed in black. All edges trimmed.

Contains a reference to two works: a watercolor and a gouache and ink, p. [14]. The watercolor is reproduced in black and white, p. [15].

Publication: 2,000 copies in November 1971, at $2.00.

B26   *The Eye of the Heart* (1973)

[device] | THE | EYE OF THE HEART | SHORT STORIES | FROM LATIN AMERICA | edited by Barbara Howes | THE BOBBS-MERRILL COMPANY, INC. | *Indianapolis / New York*

[i–viii] ix–xiv [xv–xvi], 1–415 [416]. 9¼ × 6 in. Yellow paper on boards; stamped in red on spine. White endpapers. All edges trimmed. Yellow dust jacket with red and green detail; printed in red, yellow, and white on spine, white and yellow on the front and black on the back.

Contains EB's translations of two stories by Clarice Lispector: "The Smallest Woman in the World," pp. 320–325, and "Marmosets," pp. 326–328 (**C132, C134**).

Publication: 5,500 copies on August 24, 1973, at $10.95.

B27   *Preferences* (1974)

[double rule] | PREFERENCES | *51 American poets* | *choose poems from their own work* | *and from the past* | *commentary on the choices* | *and an introduction by* | RICHARD HOWARD | *photographs of the poets by* | THOMAS VICTOR | THE VIKING PRESS · NEW YORK | [double rule]

[i–iv] v–xi [xii], [1–2] 3–6 [7–324 (the pagination proceeds as follows: each poet is introduced by a half title, recto, with a photograph, verso, and these pages are unnumbered; all pages containing poems and commentaries are numbered)]. 9¼ × 8¼ in. Red and black marbleized vinyl front and back; black cloth stamped in silver and red on spine. Yellowish white endpapers. All edges trimmed. White dust jacket printed in black, brown, and red.

Contains "In the Waiting Room," pp. 27–28 (**C148**), followed by George Herbert's "Love Unknown," pp. 29–30. Both poems were selected by Miss Bishop for this anthology.

Publication: 4,400 copies on February 20, 1974, at $17.50.

B28 *A Joseph Cornell Album* (1974)

[two pages] A JOSEPH CORNELL–ALBUM | Dore Ashton |
[drawing] | WITH SPECIAL CONTRIBUTIONS BY JOHN
ASHBERY [device] PETER BAZELEY [device] | [device] ELIZA-
BETH BISHOP [device] DENISE HARE [device] RICHARD
HOWARD [device] – [device] STANLEY KUNITZ [device]
JONAS MEKAS [device] DUANE MICHALS [device] JOHN
BERNARD MYERS [device] OCTAVIO PAZ [device] TERRY
SCHUTTÉ | [device] – [device] | AND ASSORTED EPHEM-
ERA [device] READINGS [device] DECORATIONS [device] |
AND REPRODUCTIONS OF WORKS BY JOSEPH CORNELL
| THE VIKING PRESS NEW YORK

[i–iv] v–vii [viii] ix–xiv [xv–xvi], 1–111 [112–113] 114–125 [126–128]
129–153 [154–155] 156–167 [168–169] 170–217 [218–219] 220–233
[234] 235–240. 8¾ × 9½ in. Blue boards, dark blue cloth spine stamped
in silver front and spine. White endpapers. All edges trimmed. Blue dust
jacket printed in orange, white, and black with a multi-colored picture
on front.

Contains EB's translation of Octavio Paz's "Objects and Apparitions,"
pp. 217–218 (**C161**).

Publication: 4,000 copies on November 18, 1974, at $15.00.

B29 *Self Portrait* (1976)

[rule] | SELF-PORTRAIT | [rule] | Book People Picture Them-
selves | *From the collection of* | BURT BRITTON | *Random House*
[publisher's device] *New York* | [rule]

[i–xvi], [1–2] 3–73 [74] 75–81 [82] 83–131 [132] 133–149 [150]
151–163 [164] 165–185 [186] 187–196 [197–198] 199–225 [226]
227–259 [260] 261–271 [272]. 6⅜ × 9½ in. Black boards with black
linen on spine; blind stamped on front and stamped in gold on spine.
White endpapers. All edges trimmed. Dust jacket front and back, white
printed in yellow, white, black, and red, with the names of the contributors; spine, black printed in yellow and white.

Paper Issue: 6⅛ × 9¼ in. Stiff glazed wrapper the same as the dust jacket of the hardbound.

Contains EB's self-portrait, p. 84.

Publication: 1,500 hardbound copies at $12.50 and 12,000 paper copies at $6.95.

Dust Jacket Comments

Bb1 *A Cage of Spines* (1958)

A | CAGE | OF | SPINES | [device] | *by* | *May* | *Swenson* | *Rinehart & Company, Inc.* | *NEW YORK TORONTO* | [device]

[1–8] 9–96. 8½ × 5⅞ in. Black cloth cover stamped in white on spine. White endpapers. Top and bottom edges trimmed; fore edges rough trimmed. Dust jacket, yellow and black printed in yellow, black, and white, front and spine; white printed in black on back.

Contribution on the front flap of dust jacket: ' "Miss Swenson looks, and sees, | and rejoices in what she sees. | Her poems are varied, energetic | and full of a directness and optimism | that are unusual in these days | of formulated despair and/or careful | stylishness." ELIZABETH BISHOP'.

Publication: issued September 8, 1958, at $3.75.

Bb2 *Life Studies* (1959)

[black printed in white; drawing by Frank Parker] | LIFE STUDIES | ROBERT LOWELL | Farrar, Straus and Cudahy | New York

[i–viii], [1–2] 3–8 [9–10] 11–46 [47–48] 49–55 [56–58] 59–90. 8⅝ × 5⅝ in. Green cloth cover stamped in black on spine. Beige endpapers. All edges trimmed; top edge stained green. Black and white dust jacket printed in black, white, and green.

Contribution on dust wrapper flaps, front and back: 'A statement about this book | by Elizabeth Bishop: | *"As a child, I used to look at my* | *grandfather's Bible under a powerful read-|ing glass. The letters assembled* | *beneath the* | *lens were suddenly like a Lowell poem, as* | *big as life and as* | *alive, and rainbow-edged.* | *It seemed to illuminate as it magnified; it* | *could also be used as a burning-glass.* | *[¶] This new book begins on Robert* | *Lowell's now-familiar trumpet-notes (see* | Inauguration Day), *then* | *with the auto-|biographical group called* Life Studies *the* | *tone changes. In* | *these poems, heart-break-|ing, shocking, grotesque and gentle, the* | *unhes-* | *itant attack, the imagery and con-|struction, are as brilliant as ever, but the* | *mood is nostalgic and the meter is refined.* | *A poem like* My Last | Afternoon with Uncle | Devereux Winslow, *or* Skunk Hour, *can* | [back flap] *tell us as much about the state of society* | *as a volume of Henry* | James *at his best.* | *[¶] Whenever I read a poem by Robert* | *Lowell I have* | *a chilling sensation of here-|and-now, of exact contemporaneity: more* | *aware of those 'ironies of American His-|tory,' grimmer about them, and yet* | *hope-|ful. If more people read poetry, if it were* | *more exportable and* | *translatable, surely his* | *poems would go far towards changing, or* | *at* | *least unsettling, minds made up against* | *us. Somehow or other, by fair* | *means or* | *foul, and in the middle of our worst century* | *so far, we have* | *produced a magnificent* | *poet."'*.

Publication: 4,300 copies on April 11, 1959, at $3.50.

Note: an abstract from the comment is reprinted as an advertisement for *Life Studies* on the back of the dust jacket of Lowells's *Imitations*, Farrar, Straus and Cudahy, 1961: 'ELIZABETH BISHOP: "Somehow or other . . . in the middle | of our worst century so far, we have produced a magnificent | poet." ' The comment appears in full on the back of the dust jacket of Lowells's *Notebook 1967–68*, Farrar, Straus and Giroux, 1969.

Bb3 *O to Be a Dragon* (1959)

O TO BE A DRAGON | *Marianne Moore* | THE VIKING PRESS | *New York · 1959*

[i–ii], [1–8] 9–37 [38]. 9$\frac{9}{16}$ × 6$\frac{3}{8}$ in. Blue paper-covered boards front and back; gray cloth spine stamped in silver. Gray endpapers. All edges trimmed. Gray dust jacket printed in blue.

Contribution on back of dust jacket: '*Elizabeth Bishop:* "As far as I know, Miss Marianne Moore | is the World's Greatest Living Observer." '

Publication: 5,000 copies on September 17, 1959, at $2.75.

Bb4 *To Mix with Time* (1963)

TO | MIX | WITH | TIME | *New and Selected Poems* | MAY SWENSON | *New York* | CHARLES SCRIBNER'S SONS

[i–iv] v–viii, [1–2] 3–18 [19–20] 21–44 [45–46] 47–65 [66–68] 69–81 [82–84] 85–101 [102–104] 105–118 [119–120] 121–140 [141–142] 143–164 [165–166] 167–183 [184]. 8¼ × 5⅝ in. Green cloth cover stamped in black on spine. White endpapers. All edges trimmed. White dust jacket printed in green and black.

Contribution on the back flap of dust wrapper: 'Elizabeth Bishop: | [¶] "Miss Swenson is one of the few good | poets who write good poems about na-|ture, and really about nature, not just | comparing it to states of mind or society. | She has always reminded me a little of | John Clare. A great part of one's pleasure | in her work is in *her* pleasure; she has | directness, affection, and a rare and reas-|suring ungrudgingness. When she turns | her John Clare-like gaze on New York | City she reacts just as ungrudgingly. In | this volume Miss Swenson goes on a | Grand Tour. If you have thought that no | one could ever again react as originally | and, above all, simply, as though she were | the first tourist to see the Pantheon, say, | or the Arno—you should buy and read | this book." '

Publication: issued January 29, 1963, at $3.50.

Bb5 *Golden State* (1973)

GOLDEN | STATE | *by* | FRANK BIDART | *with a note by Richard Howard* | GEORGE BRAZILLER | *New York*

[i–iv] v [vi] vii–ix [x], [1–2] 3–8 [9–10] 11–39 [40–42] 43–50 [51–52]. 8⅞ × 5⁹⁄₁₆ in. Gold cloth cover stamped in gold on spine. Yellowish white endpapers, matching the paper used to print the book. All edges trimmed. White dust jacket printed in black, gold, and white.

Paper Issue: 8%₁₆ × 5⅜ in. Stiff glazed wrapper the same as the dust jacket of the hardbound.

Contribution on back of dust jacket: 'Just possibly, Frank Bidart has achieved, in his first book, | exactly what all young poets would like to: he has discovered | and brought together a set of images, emotionally disturbing, | apparently disparate, but in combination having the un-canny | power of illuminating the poet's personal history and History | itself, literary life and plain Life, at the same time. | —ELIZABETH BISHOP'.

Publication: 500 hardbound copies at $5.95 and 1,500 paper copies at $2.95 on June 18, 1973.

Bb6   *Radiation* (1973)

Radiation | *Sandra McPherson* | [publisher's device] | *The Ecco Press New York*

[i–xii], 1–68. 8¾ × 5½ in. Yellow cloth cover stamped in gold on spine. Yellowish white endpapers. Fore edges trimmed, top and bottom edges rough trimmed. Dust jacket front and spine black printed in yellow and white; back, white printed in black.

Paper Issue: 8⁷⁄₁₆ × 5⅜ in. Stiff, glazed paper wrapper the same as dust jacket of the hardbound.

Contribution on the back of dust jacket: 'It's like turning the light switch off, and there in the | dark—reality: all kinds of likely and unlikely things, | incandescent on their own, beginning to stir and | breathe. All that really needs to be said about | Sandra McPherson's new poems is that they are | very, very good—original, surprising, and *clean*— | a delight and refreshment in the tedium of irony, | confession and cuteness of contemporary verse. | The title of the collection, *Radiation*, is beautifully | suitable. | —Elizabeth Bishop'.

Publication: 1,500 cloth copies at $6.95 and 3,000 paper copies at $2.95 in September 1973.

C

Contributions to Periodicals

C1   "Behind Stowe." *The Blue Pencil* (Walnut Hill School), 11 (December 1927), 10.

C2   "To a Tree." *The Blue Pencil*, 11 (December 1927), 10.

C3   "The Stomach—An Allegory" (article). *The Blue Pencil*, 11 (December 1927), 25–27.

C4   "In Appreciation of Shelley's Poems" (general book review). *The Blue Pencil*, 11 (December 1927), 30–31.

C5   "Roof-Tops" (article). *The Blue Pencil*, 11 (March 1928), 2–3.

C6   "Storm" (article). *The Blue Pencil*, 11 (March 1928), 22–23.

C7   "Thunder." *The Blue Pencil*, 11 (June 1928), 24.

C8   "The Three Wells" (play). *The Blue Pencil*, 11 (June 1928), 31–36.

C9   "Sonnet." *The Blue Pencil*, 11 (June 1928), 45.

C10   "Giant Weather" (article). *The Blue Pencil*, 12 (December 1928), 4–6.

C11   "Imber Nocturnus." *The Blue Pencil*, 12 (December 1928), 16.

C12   "Picking Mushrooms" (story). *The Blue Pencil*, 12 (December 1928), 18–20.

C13   Review of *Green Mansions*. *The Blue Pencil*, 12 (December 1928), 27–28.

C14   Review of *The Buck in the Snow*. *The Blue Pencil*, 12 (December 1928), 30.

C15   "For C.W.B." *The Blue Pencil*, 12 (April 1929), 14.

C16   "The Wave." *The Blue Pencil*, 12 (April 1929), 17.

C17   "Into the Mountain" (story). *The Blue Pencil*, 12 (April 1929), 26–29.

C18   Review of *The Letters of Katherine Mansfield*. *The Blue Pencil*, 12 (April 1929), 39.

C19   "On Being Alone" (article). *The Blue Pencil*, 12 (June 1929), 18.

C20 "I Meet a Knight" (story). *The Blue Pencil*, 12 (June 1929), 25–30.

C21 Review of *The Pathway* by Henry Williamson. *The Blue Pencil*, 12 (June 1929), 50.

C22 "The Pencil Sharpener" (article). *The Blue Pencil*, 13 (December 1929), 3–4.

C23 "A Mouse and Mice" (article). *The Blue Pencil*, 13 (December 1929), 18–19.

C24 "A Flight of Fancy" (story). *The Blue Pencil*, 13 (December 1929), 22–26.

C25 "The Thumb" (story). *The Blue Pencil*, 13 (April 1930), 6–9.

C26 "The Pencil Sharpener" (article). *The Blue Pencil*, 13 (June 1930), 3–4.

C27 Unsigned. "The Flood." *Con Spirito* (Vassar), 1 (February 1933), 1.

C28 Unsigned. "Then Came the Poor" (story). *Con Spirito*, 1 (February 1933), 2. Reprinted in *The Magazine*, 1 (March 1934), 105–110.

C29 "Chimney Sweepers" (story). *Vassar Review*, 19 (Spring 1933), 8–10, 36.

C30 Unsigned. "A Word with You." *Con Spirito*, 1 (April 1933), 2.

C31 Unsigned. "Hymn to the Virgin." *Con Spirito*, 1 (April 1933), 3. Reprinted in *The Magazine*, 1 (April 1934), 161.
1   quick,]   ~∧ *The Magazine*
3   baby brood]   baby-brood *The Magazine*
4   Strawberry-ice-cream-colored]   Strawberry ice-cream colored *The Magazine*
4   ascending,]   ~∧ *The Magazine*
8   moths,]   ~∧ *The Magazine*
12   paraphernalia,]   ~∧ *The Magazine*
36   Omega–]   ~, *The Magazine*
40   nickels,–]   ~,∧ *The Magazine*
42   You]   The *The Magazine*
42   not!]   ~? *The Magazine*
43   close]   draw *The Magazine*
44   rest . . . .]   ~. *The Magazine*

C32 Unsigned. "Seven-Days Monologue" (story). *Con Spirito*, 1 (April 1933), 3–4.

C33 "Time's Andromedas" (article). *Vassar Journal of Undergraduate Studies*, 7 (1933), 102–120.

C34 "Mr. Pope's Garden" (story). *Vassar Review*, 20 (Summer 1933), 9–10, 24, 27.

C35 Unsigned. "Three Sonnets for Eyes." *Con Spirito*, 2 (November 1933), 3.

C36 "Some Dreams They Forgot." *Vassar Review*, 22 (December 1933), 15. CP.

first letter of the first word in each line capitalized] ∼ *not capitalized* CP

2 guessed] could guess CP

2 black;] ∼, CP

4 new] the ∼ CP

5 Also∧ . . . fell; night- . . . eaves∧] ∼, . . . ∼. Night- . . . eaves, CP

12 left, or,] ∼?∼∧CP

unsigned] *signed: 1933* CP

13 Columbine] columbine CP

14 at eight o'clock] by eight CP

C37 "Valentine." *Vassar Review*, 23 (February 1934), 1. **B2**.

13 sashes,] ∼∧**B2**

C38 "Gerald Manley Hopkins: Notes on Timing in His Poetry" (article). *Vassar Review*, 23 (February 1934), 5–7.

EB to MM, April 2, 1935: It has been very strange finding in the Hopkins' letters that he grew more and more absorbed in music, and mentions some of the very things I've been studying. His own ideas about composition seem almost to forecast some of Schönberg—I wonder, if I re-wrote my paper on Hopkins, if it would be asking too much to ask you to look at it again?

C39 "Valentine II." *Vassar Review*, 23 (February 1934), 14. **B2**.

C40 "The Last Animal" (story). *Vassar Review*, 25 (April 1934), 3–5, 18–19.

C41 Review of *Journey to the End of Night*, by Louis Ferdinand Céline, tr. John H. P. Marks. *Vassar Review*, 25 (May 1934), 25–26.

C42 "Dimensions for a Novel" (article). *Vassar Journal of Undergraduate Studies*, 8 (May 1934), 95–103.

C43 "The Imaginary Iceberg." *Direction: A Quarterly Review of Literature*, 1 (April/June 1935), 135. **B8, B9**, NS, Po, CP / P, S.

first letter of the first word in each line capitalized] ∼ *not capitalized* NS+

7 ship's] ships' NS (first printing), Po

3 stock still] stock-still NS+

28 Goodbye . . . goodbye] Good-bye . . . good-bye NS+

C44   "The Man-Moth." *Life and Letters To-day*, 14 (Spring 1936), 92–93. NS, Po, CP / P, S.

first letter of the first word in each line capitalized]   ~ *not capitalized* NS+

13   of building]   of the buildings Po+
17   facades]   façades NS+
36   window‸]   ~, NS+
38   as disease]   as a disease Po+

C45   "Casabianca." *New Democracy*, 6 (April 1936), 36. B3, NS, Po, CP.

first letter of the first word in each line capitalized]   ~ *not capitalized* NS+

C46   "The Colder the Air." *New Democracy*, 6 (April 1936), 36. B3, NS, Po, CP / P, S.

first letter of the first word in each line capitalized]   ~ *not capitalized* NS+

C47   "The Gentleman of Shalot." *New Democracy*, 6 (April 1936), 36. B3, NS, Po, CP.

The Gentleman of Shalot]   The Gentlemen of Shalot Po

C48   "The Weed." *Forum and Century*, 97 (February 1937), 114. B7, NS, Po, CP / P.

first letter of the first word in each line capitalized]   ~ *not capitalized* NS+

3   bower.)]   ~). NS+   34   cascades,)]   ~‸) NS+
14   sleep,]   ~. NS+   46   itself,]   ~‸Po+

Note: Marianne Moore retyped "The Weed," as she did at least four of Bishop's early poems.

   EB to MM, October 18, 1936: P. S.—I have just this minute received word from Roger Roughton [editor of *Contemporary Poetry and Prose*] that he will not accept the WEED this time either.

   EB to MM, October 27, 1936: P. S. I must add my gratitude for all the time you have spent on the WEED. I don't see how you could bear to copy it, the way you did, and I am extremely grateful. I am afraid my ungraciousness appears here the same way it did as regards the story: I sent Mr. Zabel [Morton Dauwen Zabel, editor of *Poetry*] your very superior copy, with "neither" in it [l. 26], and "out of" [l. 20]—both of which I thank you for very much, as for the other suggestions I didn't accept. I am not sure why I didn't, because I make no pretense of comparing my "ear" to your own. I suppose one is very selfish in one's conception of the "picture".

   EB to MM, February 4, 1937: I am sorry I let *The Weed* appear in the *Forum*—I don't like the other poems at all and even my own, there, although I am sorry for such conceit, too.

C49 "The Baptism" (story). *Life and Letters To-day*, 16 (Spring 1937), 71–78.

C50 "Two Mornings and Two Evenings": "Paris, 7 A.M." *Poetry*, 50 (July 1937), 181–182. NS, Po, CP.

first letter of the first word in each line capitalized]   ~ *not capitalized*
  NS+

5   their]   the NS+

14   stare-inside]   stare inside NS+

16   there.]   ~. NS+

22   only be]   turned to NS+

23   Be]   and NS+

a space between l.25 and l.26]   *no space* NS+

32   say: . . . below.]   ~; . . . ~, NS+

33   snow.]   ~? NS+

EB to MM, September 29, 1936: I am enclosing a slightly corrected version of PARIS, 7 A.M.—I do not know whether you will think it fit to send to POETRY as it is now or not, or whether you had rather wait until I have finished one or two more—to which I am lending my efforts now—I am sorry I am being so obstinate about "apartments". To me that word suggests so strongly the structure of the houses, later referred to, and suggests a "cut off" made of existence so well—that I don't want to change it unless you feel it would mean a great improvement.

C51 "Two Mornings and Two Evenings": "A Miracle for Breakfast." *Poetry*, 50 (July 1937), 182–184. Reprinted in *Poetry*, 121 (October 1972), 3–4. NS, Po, CP / S.

printed with an epigraph: Miracles enable us to judge of | doctrine, and
  doctrine enables | us to judge of miracles.]   *printed without an epi-*
  graph NS+

first letter of the first word in each line capitalized]   ~ *not capitalized*
  NS+

11   each.]   ~, NS+

14   towards]   toward NS+

15   the]   a NS+

32   by a miracle]   a miracle NS (first printing)

EB to MM, September 15, 1936: I realize there are awful faults— one being vague, another an extremely impolite, if true, display of your "influence"; the sestina is just a sort of stunt.

EB to MM, January 5, 1937: You are no comfort to me, at all, Miss

Moore, the way you inevitably light on just those things I knew I shouldn't have let go—I must be unusually insensitive to be able to bear being brought face to face with my conscience this way over and over. I mean in A MIRACLE FOR BREAKFAST. I knew I should not have let the "bitterly" and "very hot" in the second stanza go. It is as yet unsolved. The boisterousness of "gallons of coffee" I want to overlook because I like "gallons" being near "galleries". And the "crumb" and "sun" is of course its greatest fault. It seems to me that there are two ways possible for a sestina—one is to use unusual words as terminations, in which case they would have to be used differently as often as possible—as you say, "change of scale". That would make a very highly seasoned kind of poem. And the other way is to use as colorless words as possible—like Sydney, so that it becomes less of a trick and more of a natural theme and variations. I guess I have tried to do both at once. It is probably just an excuse, but sometimes I think about certain things that without one particular fault they would be without the means of existence. I feel a little that way about "sun" and "crumb!"—but I know at the same time it is only justified about someone else's work.

EB to MM, January 19, 1937 (after signature): I have changed,— very feebly—the second line of the 2nd stanza of A MIRACLE, etc., to:

> In the bitter cold we hoped that the coffee
> Would be very hot, seeing that the sun—

C52 "Two Mornings and Two Evenings": "From the Country to the City." *Poetry*, 50 (July 1937), 184–185. NS, Po, CP / S.
first letter of the first word in each line capitalized] ~ *not capitalized* NS+
8   and.] ~, NS+
27   country-wards] countrywards NS+

EB to MM, December 5, 1936: I wanted to know if, as I feel, it may possibly be an example of "rainsoaked foppishness".—In the last part I am referring to the peculiar effect of the headlights on the telephone wires ahead, driving at night.

C53 "Two Morning and Two Evenings": "Song." *Poetry*, 50 (July 1937), 185. CP.
first letter of the first word in each line capitalized] ~ *not capitalized* CP
8   freighter] freighters CP
9   goes] go CP
unsigned] *signed: 1937* CP

C54 "The Hanging of the Mouse" (story). *Life and Letters To-day*, 17 (Autumn 1937), 111–112. CP.

EB to MM, February 4, 1937: I once hung Minnow's artificial mouse on a string to a chair back, without thinking what I was doing—it looked very sad.

C55 "The Sea and Its Shore" (story). *Life and Letters To-day*, 17 (Winter 1937), 103–108. B4.

EB to MM, January 5, 1937: This morning I have been working on THE SEA & ITS SHORE—or rather, making use of your and your mother's work—and I am suddenly afraid that at the end I have stolen something from THE FRIGATE PELICAN. I say: "Large flakes of blackened paper, still sparkling red at the edges, flew into the sky. While his eyes could follow them, he had never seen such clever, quivering manoeuvres." It was not until I began seeing pelicans that my true source occurred to me. I know you speak of the flight like "charred paper", and use the word manoeuvres. I am afraid it is almost criminal. I haven't the book here and I wonder if you will tell me just how guilty I am and forgive what was really unconscious. When I think of the care and time that you and your mother have taken with that poor story I feel that from now I shall be able to notice my own roughness and lack of natural correctness better. I have taken over, or gobbled up like a pelican, everything you suggested except one: "It is an extremely picturesque scene. . ." You say you feel it to be too "automatic". In a way, that was what I meant it to be—I was, I suppose, making fun of an automatic reaction to the scene I was describing and I wanted, as the only "moral" to the story, to contradict, as quietly as possible, the automatic, banal thing that one might have said: "How *picturesque*—He looks like a Rembrandt!" That is, the conclusion of the sentence, "but in many ways not" is really thought of as being spoken in a different tone of voice. However, if this over-subtlety (and I'm afraid, superiority) on my part did not make itself plain to you there must be something very wrong and I'm going to try to change it and convey the idea a little more clearly.

C56 "Love Lies Sleeping." *Partisan Review*, 4 (January 1938), 14–15. B10, NS, Po, CP.

first letter of the first word in each line capitalized] ~*not capitalized* NS+

16 facade] façade NS+

28 again,] ~. CP

33 back] backs NS+

34 thread-like] threadlike CP

40   water-melon]   watermelon NS+
53   one∧ or several∧]   ~, ~, NS+

C57   "In Prison" (story). *Partisan Review*, 4 (March 1938), 3–10. **B10**.

EB to MM, January 31, 1938: I finished a story a few days ago which I wanted to send to you to see what you thought of it—but I had just received a letter from the "Partisan Review" asking for a story by February 1st, if possible. I sent it to them and now of course regret it very much and hope they will send it back. My motives were doubly corrupt: they are going to have a $100. "contest" and I thought I should like to try. It is called "In Prison" and is another one of these horrible "fable" ideas that seem to obsess me—

C58   "The Unbeliever." *Partisan Review*, 5 (August/September 1938), 63. NS, Po, CP / P.

first letter of the first word in each line capitalized]   ~ *not capitalized* NS+

6   there.]   ~, NS+   18   said,]   ~: NS+
14   Secured]   Secure NS+   26   diamond]   diamonds NS+

C59   "Poem [Late Air]." *Partisan Review*, 5 (August/September 1938), 64. NS, Po, CP.

Poem]   Late Air NS+

first letter of the first word in each line capitalized]   ~ *not capitalized* NS+

7   Navy-Yard]   Navy Yard CP
signed: Key West]   *unsigned* NS+

C60   "Quai d'Orleans." *Partisan Review*, 5 (August/September 1938), 64. NS, Po, CP.

first letter of the first word in each line capitalized]   ~ *not capitalized* NS+

no dedication]   *for Margaret Miller* CP

13   The]   And NS+   23   itself.]   ~∧NS+
15   seas']   sea's CP

C61   "Sleeping on the Ceiling." *Life and Letters To-day*, 19 (October 1938), 47. NS, Po, CP.

first letter of the first word in each line capitalized]   ~ *not capitalized* NS+

6, 11   wall-paper]   wallpaper NS+
15   oh∧]   ~, NS+

EB to MM, February 14, 1938: I have just had another letter from Miss Norman [Dorothy S. Norman, editor of *Twice a Year*], and I am wondering if you think that to send the two little "sleeping" poems to her would be all right.

C62 "Sleeping Standing Up." *Life and Letters To-day*, 19 (November 1938), 55. NS, Po, CP, P.

first letter of the first word in each line capitalized] ~ *not capitalized* NS+

15 a] the NS+

C63 "Florida." *Partisan Review*, 6 (Winter 1939), 40–41. NS, Po, CP / S.

first letter of the first word in each line capitalized] ~ *not capitalized* NS+

6 Dotted] dotted. NS+

9 unseen,] ~. NS+

12, 22 Pelicans] pelicans NS+

32 circles,] ~. NS+

38 fire-flies] fireflies CP

40 Cold-white] Cold white NS+

46 warning,] ~– CP

EB to MM, February 4, 1937: The purpose of my trip to Fort Myers was to see Ross Allen wrestle with a live alligator and give a lecture on, and exhibit of, snakes. . . . The part of the show devoted to the alligator was memorable chiefly because Mr. Allen wanted to creep up on it (in a big swimming pool) unnoticed, and yet go on with the lecture—so he slid into the water and kept right on talking. It was quite a sight to see his large, solemn baby-face apparently floating bodiless on the surface of the water while from it came his imitations of the alligator's calls: the "hello", the love-call, the warning and the social call. [¶] . . . and afterwards we had dinner with Ross Allen, whose table-conversation consists of imitations of animals and birds. "Now *this*," he would say "can be heard for several miles," and we would all murmur, "Pretty."

C64 "Gregorio Valdes, 1879–1939" (article). *Partisan Review*, 6 (Summer 1939), 91–97 (photographs also by EB).

Note: EB remembers that a Spanish translation was reprinted with her photographs in a Cuban magazine about 1940.

C65 "Cirque d'Hiver." *New Yorker*, 15 (Jan. 27, 1940), 23. NS, Po, CP / P, S.

first letter of the first word in each line capitalized] ~ *not capitalized* NS+

EB to MM, November 20, 1939: The NEW YORKER took the little poem about the toy horse—only I changed the title to Cirque d'Hiver. They want some more—

C66 "The Fish." *Partisan Review*, 7 (March/April 1940), 107–108.

NS, Po, CP / P, S.
7   hung,]   ~ˌ NS+
11, 13   wall-paper]   wallpaper CP
49   lip,]   ~— NS+
50   that grim]   grim NS+
50   almost-weapon—]   and weapon-like, NS+
55   fast]   firmly NS+
74   gunnels,]   ~ˌ NS+

 EB to MM, February 19, 1940: And thank you for the marvellous postcard, and the very helpful comments on the Fish. I did as you suggested about everything except "breathing in" (if you can remember that) which I decided to leave as it was. "Lousy" is now "infested", and "gunwales"—which I had meant to be pronounced "gunn'ls", is "gunnels"—which is also correct, according to the dictionary, and makes it plainer. I left off the outline of capitals, too, and feel very ADVANCED.

C67   "Song: Letter to New York [Letter to N.Y.]." *Harper's Bazaar,* 2742 (Sept. 15, 1940), 102. **B7,** CS, CP / P.

Song: Letter to New York]   Letter to N.Y. CS+

first letter of the first word in each line capitalized]   ~ *not capitalized* CS+

no dedication]   *for Louise Crane* CP

C68   "Roosters." *New Republic,* 104 (April 21, 1941), 547–548. **B6,** NS, Po, CP / P, S.
8   back-yard]   backyard CP
15   hen-house]   henhouse NS+
40   glass-headed]   glass headed NS, Po
41   copper-greens]   copper greens NS+
54   commands,]   ~ˌ NS+
60   fighting-blood]   fighting blood NS
device deviding stanza 26 from stanza 27 and stanza 39 from stanza 40]   *omitted* NS+
85   scripture]   sculpture NS+
94   *Gallus Canit]*   gallus canit NS+
95   *Flet]*   *flet* NS+
116   deny,"]   ~ˌ" CP
unsigned]   *signed:* 1941 NS

 EB to MM, October 17, [1940] (*concerning a copy of "Roosters," which Moore retyped and retitled "The Cock"*): What I'm about to say, I'm afraid, will sound like ELIZABETH KNOWS BEST . . .

However, I *have* changed to small initial letters! & I have made several other of your corrections and suggestions, & left out 1 of the same stanzas that you did. But I can't seem to bring myself to give up the set form, which I'm afraid you think fills the poem with redundancies, etc. I feel that the rather rattle-trap rhythm is appropriate—maybe I can explain it. [¶] I cherish my "water-closet" and other sordidities because I want to emphasize the essential baseness of militarism. In the 1st part I was thinking of Key West, and also of those aerial views of dismal little towns in Finland & Norway, when the Germans took over, and their atmosphere of poverty. That's why, although I see what *you* mean, I want to keep "tin rooster" instead of "gold", and not to use "fastidious beds". And for the same reason I want to keep as the title the rather contemptuous word ROOSTERS rather than the more classical COCK; and I want to repeat the "gun-metal". (I also had in mind the violent roosters Picasso did in connection with his GUERNICA picture.) [¶] About the "glass-headed pins": I felt the roosters to be placed here and there (by their various crowings) like the pins that point out war-projects on a map—maybe I haven't made it clear enough. [¶] And I wanted to keep "to see the end" in quotes because, although it may not be generally recognized, I have always felt that expression used of Peter in the Bible, to be extremely poignant. [¶] It has been so hard to decide what to do, and I know that esthetically you are quite right, but I can't bring myself to sacrifice what (I think) is a very important "violence" of tone—which I feel to be helped by what *you* must feel to be just a bad case of the *Threes*. It makes me feel like a wonderful Klee picture I saw at his show the other day, "The Man of Confusion".

Note: on a postcard, August 12, 1977, to CWM, EB identified the source of "to see the end" as Matthew 24:58, King James Version.

C69 "Jeronymo's House [Jerónimo's House]." *Partisan Review*, 8 (September/October 1941), 382. NS, Po, CP / S.

Jeronymo's House]   Jerónimo's House NS+

fn. *for José Marti*: a Cuban patriot]   *no footnote* Po+

11   verandah]   veranda NS+

30   wall]   walls NS+

42   hook‸]   ~, NS+

44   re-painted]   repainted NS+

60   things‸]   ~, Po+

61   and no more]   and not much more Po+

EB to MM, February 19, 1940 (there is a typescript of "Jerónimo's

House," titled "José's House," at the bottom of which is a hand-colored drawing): I am enclosing another poem that I'm afraid isn't very good—I just can't tell any more—perhaps if I think about your maxim for Key West I may be able to improve it in some way. I thought something *jiggeldy* would suit the Cuban houses, but I don't know. They pay from $1.00 to $2.00 a week rent . . . .

C70 "Cootchie." *Partisan Review,* 8 (September/October 1941), 384. NS, Po, CP / S.

16 light-house] lighthouse NS+

EB to MM, February 26, 1940: I want to do what a young man here calls a "tript-itch" of Key West poems. I am enclosing another one that may be banal. I can't decide. Maybe you will remember Cootchie—I don't know what Miss Lula is going to do without her, she had lived with her 35 years.

C71 "Sea-Scape [Seascape]." *Partisan Review,* 8 (September/October 1941), 384–385. NS, Po, CP.

Sea-Scape] Seascape
1 sea-scape] seascape NS+
2 sidewise] side-wise NS+
6 dropping] droppings NS+
8 down] and down NS+
13, 19 Heaven] heaven NS+
16 "lives on his nerves,"] '~~~~,' NS; ^~~~~,^ Po+

C72 "Songs for a Colored Singer." *Partisan Review,* 11 (Fall 1944), 429–432. NS, Po, CP / S.

I.] II.^ NS+
  5 'cause this occasion's all his fault.] this occasion's all his fault. CP
  Note: the alteration of stanzaic form that occurs in *The Complete Poems* with this change in diction was not intended by Miss Bishop when she updated the language. It is a misprint.
  7 He's drinking in the warm pink glow] across the street at Flossie's place. NS+
  8 across the street at Flossie's place,] He's drinking in the warm pink glow NS+
  fn. *no footnote*] *footnote for piccolo: Jukebox* CP
II.] I.^ NS+
  5 neighbor's] neighbors NS+
  15 hard.] ~. CP
  16 that all . . . cents.] What have . . . cents? CP
  17 's a pile] —A pile CP

22 will answer] answers Po+
III.] III.NS+
IV.] IV.NS+
  4 leaves.] ~? NS+
  8 tears.] ~? NS+

C73 "Anaphora." *Partisan Review*, 12 (Fall 1945), 480. NS, Po, CP.
no dedication] in memory of Majorie Carr Stevens CP
  8 made] meant NS+

C74 "Little Exercise at 4 A.M. [Little Exercise]." *New Yorker*, 21 (Feb. 2, 1946), 22. NS, Po, CP / P.
Little Exercise at 4 A.M.] Little Exercise NS+
no dedication] for Thomas Edwards Wanning CP
  5 lightning,] ~.NS+
 12 fish skeletons] fish-skeletons NS+
 14 sidewalks,] ~.NS+
 17 battle scenes] battle-scenes NS+
 19 rowboat] row-boat NS+

C75 "Chemin de Fer." *New Yorker*, 22 (April 13, 1946), 95. NS, Po, CP.
  6 scrub pine] scrub-pine NS+
  9 lives.] ~, NS+
 13 shotgun] shot-gun NS+

C76 "Large Bad Picture." *New Yorker*, 22 (April 20, 1946), 36. NS, Po, CP / P, S.
  7 pale-blue] pale blue NS+
 16 burned] burnt NS+
 18 semitranslucent] semi-translucent NS+
 20 "n"s,] n's, NS; *n's.* Po+

C77 "Argument." *Partisan Review*, 14 (January/February 1947), 58. CS, CP.
  6 endlessly,] ~.CS+

C78 "Faustina, or Rock Roses." *Nation*, 164 (Feb. 22, 1947), 214. CS, CP / P, S.
  6 rose-like] roselike CP
  9 floor-boards] floorboards CS+
 20 eighty watt] eighty-watt CS+
 48 says.] says, CS+
Note: a typescript and ten revisions are in Houghton Library.

C79 "Varick Street." *Nation*, 164 (March 15, 1947), 308. CS, CP / S.
 26 suppose,] ~; CS+

C80 "At the Fishhouses." *New Yorker*, 23 (Aug. 9, 1947), 30. CS, CP /P, S.
  4 invisible,] ~ˌCS+
a space dividing l. 31 from l. 32] *no space* CS+
  54 I sang him] I also sang CS+
  75 dark-gray] dark gray CS+

C81 "The Farmer's Children" (story). *Harper's Bazaar*, 2834 (February 1948), 160. **B11**.

C82 "For M.M. [Invitation to Miss Marianne Moore]." *Quarterly Review of Literature*, 4 ([Spring] 1948), 127–128. Reprinted in *Quarterly Review of Literature*, 19, nos. 1–2 (1974), 85–86; *Bryn Mawr Alumnae Bulletin*, 43 (Spring 1962), 4. CS, CP / P, S.
For M.M.] Invitation to Miss Marianne Moore CS+
fn. Suggested by a poem of Pablo Neruda] *no footnote* CS+
  19 high-light] highlight CS+
  20 cape-full] capeful CS+
  32 taxi-cabs] taxicabs CS+
  33 blowing] resounding CS+
  35 musicˌ] ~, CS+
  45 the] a CS+
Note: a typescript is in Houghton Library.

C83 "As We Like It" (article). *Quarterly Review of Literature*, 4 ([Spring] 1948), 129–135. Reprinted in *Quarterly Review of Literature*, 20, nos. 1–2 (1976), 177–183.

C84 "Over 2000 Illustrations and a Complete Concordance." *Partisan Review*, 15 (June 1948), 631–633. **B14**, CS, CP / S.
Note: when this poem was reprinted in CP, a break intended between lines 31–32 was omitted accidentally.
  42 juke-box] jukebox CP
  53 giggling,] ~ˌCS+
  65 "and," and,] ~, ~ˌCS; ~ˌ~ˌCP

C85 "A Summer's Dream." *New Yorker*, 24 (July 24, 1948), 28. CS, CP / S.

C86 Signed "Sarah Foster." "The Housekeeper" (story). *New Yorker*, 24 (Sept. 11, 1948), 56, 58, 60–61.
Note: pp. 60, 62, 64–65 in the Manhattan edition.

C87 "The Bight." *New Yorker*, 24 (Feb. 19, 1949), 30. CS, CP / P, S.
  2 White,] ~ˌCS+
  10 *claves*] claves CS+
Note: a typescript is in Houghton Library.

C88 "Cape Breton." *New Yorker*, 25 (June 18, 1949), 24. CS, CP
/ S.
  5 Baaa, Baaa] Baaa, baaa CS+
  32 the deep] deep CS+
  39 fish nets] fish-nets CS±
  43 a] his CS+
a space dividing ln. 43 from ln. 44] *no line* CS+

C89 "O Breath" [collected in "Four Poems"]. *Partisan Review*, 16
(September 1949), 894. CS, CP.
O BREATH] IV / *O Breath* CS+
  2 bored, really, blindly-veined] ~˄~˄ blindly veined CS+
  3 maybe,] ~˄CS+
  4 passes,] ~˄CS+
  5 moving,] ~˄CS+
  12 have] own CS+
  15 *line indented 7 spaces*] *no indentation* CS+

C90 Unsigned. Review of *Annie Allen* by Gwendolyn Brooks. *United
States Quarterly Book List*, 6 (March 1950), 21.

C91 "Rainbow" (tr. of Max Jacob). *Poetry*, 76 (May 1950), 83.

C92 "Patience of an Angel" (tr. of Max Jacob). *Poetry*, 76 (May
1950), 83.

C93 "Banks" (tr. of Max Jacob). *Poetry*, 76 (May 1950), 84.

C94 "Hell Is Graduated" (tr. of Max Jacob). *Poetry*, 76 (May 1950),
84–85.

C95 Unsigned. Review of *XAIPE: Seventy-one Poems* by Edward
Estlin Cummings. *United States Quarterly Book Review*, 6 (June
1950), 160–161.

C96 "Rain towards Morning" [see *Note*]. *Partisan Review*, 18 (January 1951), 41–42. CS, CP / P (II, III).
Note: poem reprinted as three poems in "Four Poems."
I] II / *Rain Towards Morning* CS+
  5 birds,] ~; CS+
  7 prison,] ~˄CS+
  8 changed] solved CS+
II] I / *Conversation* CS+
  8 half meaning] half-meaning CS+
III] III / *While Someone Telephones* CS+
  1 wasted,] ~˄CS+
  7 goes, must go, by˄] goes by, ~˄~, CS+
  7 tension,] ~; CS+

    11   soul's]   heart's CS+
    14   mean]   be CS+

Note: a typescript titled "Four Poems" is with Miss Bishop's letters to Houghton Mifflin, Houghton Library.

C97   "The Prodigal." *New Yorker*, 27 (March 17, 1951), 30. B13, CS, CP / P, S.

C98   "Insomnia." *New Yorker*, 27 (June 23, 1951), 34. CS, CP.

C99   "View of the Capitol from the Library of Congress." *New Yorker*, 27 (July 7, 1951), 17. CS, CP.

    7   brilliant]   Air Force CS+
    10   dim,]   ~ₐCS+
    15   gold dust]   gold-dust CS+
    22   *boom-boom*]   ~ — ~ CS+

C100   "What the Young Man Said to the Psalmist" (review). *Poetry*, 79 (January 1952), 212–214.

C101   "A Cold Spring (for a friend in Maryland)." *New Yorker*, 28 (May 31, 1952), 31. CS, CP / P.

    10   lowing,]   ~ₐCS+
    11   taking . . . afterbirth]   and took . . . after-birth CS+
    18   cigarette butt,]   cigarette-butt; CS+
    23   oak leaves]   oak-leaves CS+
    24   Song sparrows . . . summer,]   Song-sparrows . . . summerₐCS+
    28   whitened;]   ~, CS+
    34   bullfrogs]   bull-frogs CS+
    42   again—]   ~: CS+
    45   exactly]   —~ CS+
    46   (Later . . . higher.)]   —Later . . . ~ .ₐCS+

For a Friend in Maryland]   For Jane Dewey. Maryland. CS+

C102   "Arrival at Santos." *New Yorker*, 28 (June 21, 1952), 24. CS, QT, CP / S.

    2   horizons]   horizon CS+
    7   dishevelled]   uncertain CS+
    19 · awkwardly]   gingerly CS+
    27   bright-blue]   bright blue CS+
    31   Scotch]   bourbon QT+

unsigned]   *signed: January, 1952* QT+

C103   "The Mountain." *Poetry*, 81 (October 1952), 12. CS.

    17   demarcation]   demarcations CS
    18   sink]   fade CS
    19   blurred]   blue CS

21 down;] ~, CS
22 oh.] ~, CS
25 here] ~, CS
26 feathers . . . feathers] feather . . . feather CS
29 Bird-calls] The birdcalls CS
30 dribble and the] dwindle. The CS

EB to MM, April 11, 1953: Thank you for being nice about "The Mountain" because it really is just a "contribution"—all I could scrape up when the hat went around and I don't think much of it—I improved it some, I think, but they didn't get that version in time.

C104 "Gwendolyn" (story). *New Yorker*, 29 (June 27, 1953), 26–31.

C105 "In the Village" (story). *New Yorker*, 29 (Dec. 19, 1953), 26–34. **B18**, QT.

C106 "The Shampoo." *New Republic*, 133 (July 11, 1955), 19. CS, CP / S.

C107 "Manners (Poem for a Child of 1918)." *New Yorker*, 31 (Nov. 26, 1955), 48. QT, CP / S.

POEM FOR A CHILD OF 1918] *for a Child of 1918* QT[+]

EB to MM, February 27, 1956: I'm pleased you liked my simple-minded "Manners" poem . . . I'd like to do a whole set for a children's small book sometime

C108 "Filling Station." *New Yorker*, 31 (Dec. 10, 1955), 48. QT, CP / S.

4 surprising] disturbing QT[+]
29 Why, oh why, the table] Why the taboret QT[+]

C109 "Questions of Travel." *New Yorker*, 31 (Jan. 21, 1956), 40. QT, CP / S.

C110 "The Wit." *New Republic*, 134 (Feb. 13, 1956), 17. **B16**.

C111 "Exchanging Hats." *New World Writing*, 9 (April 1956), 128–129.

C112 "Squatter's Children." *Anhembi* (São Paulo), 22, no. 65 (April 1956), 288–289. Reprinted in *New Yorker*, 33 (March 23, 1957), 36. **B16**, QT, CP / S.

2,3 speck-like] specklike *New Yorker*[+]
12 Father's] father's *New Yorker*[+]
27 beguiled] ~, *New Yorker*[+]
fn. *printed with a long footnote in Portuguese*] *no footnote New Yorker*[+]

C113 "Manuelzinho (Brazil. A Friend of the Writer Is Speaking)." *New Yorker*, 32 (May 26, 1956), 32. QT, CP / S.

73 of] or QT

C114 "Sestina." *New Yorker*, 32 (Sept. 15, 1956), 46. QT, CP / S.
18 heartless] clever QT$^+$
19 Like a bird,] Birdlike, QT$^+$

C115 "The Manipulation of Mirrors" (review). *New Republic*, 135 (Nov. 19, 1956), 23–24.

C116 "Visits to St. Elizabeths." *Partisan Review*, 24 (Spring 1957), 185–187. **B21**, QT, CP / S.

C117 "The Armadillo–Brazil [The Armadillo]." *New Yorker*, 33 (June 22, 1957), 24. **B17**, QT, CP / S.
The Armadillo–Brazil] The Armadillo QT$^+$
no dedication] (FOR ROBERT LOWELL) QT$^+$
Note: a typescript is in Houghton Library.

C118 Abstracts "From *The Diary of 'Helena Morley.'*" *Harper's Bazaar*, 2953 (December 1957), 155–159.

C119 "Sunday, 4 A.M." *New Yorker*, 34 (Sept. 20, 1958), 42. QT, CP.
1 endless,] endless and QT$^+$
3 crucifix-] cross- QT$^+$

C120 "I Was But Just Awake" (review). *Poetry*, 93 (October 1958), 50–54.

C121 "Brazil, January 1, 1502." *New Yorker*, 35 (Jan. 2, 1960), 26. QT, CP / S.
epigraph signed: 1949] *unsigned* QT$^+$
a space dividing ln. 46 from ln. 47] *no space* QT$^+$
50 himself.] ~— QT$^+$
51 (those] .~ QT$^+$
52 other–or . . . ?),] other (or . . . ?).QT$^+$

C122 "The Riverman." *New Yorker*, 36 (April 2, 1960), 40. QT, CP / S.
one extra line of explication appears at the beginning: The *sacacas* named were famous fifty years ago.] *line omitted* QT$^+$
8 *no such line*] I got out of my hammock QT$^+$
8/9 I went] and went QT$^+$
112/113 world;] ~.. QT$^+$
122/123 alligators,] crocodiles, QT$^+$
154/155 will I] I will QT$^+$

C123 "Electrical Storm." *New Yorker*, 36 (May 14, 1960), 40. QT, CP / S.

15   until after]   until well after QT⁺

C124   "Song for a Rainy Season." *New Yorker*, 36 (Oct. 8, 1960), 40.
B19, QT, CP / S.
Song for a Rainy Season]   ~ ~ the ~ ~ QT⁺
29   love,]   ~ˌQT
34   eyes;]   ~, QT⁺
35   too indulgent, perhaps,]   to membership QT⁺
36   to]   of QT⁺
37   to booksworms,]   bookworms, QT⁺
38   moths,]   moths; with a wall QT⁺
39   and]   for QT⁺
40   maps,]   ~ ; QT⁺

C125   "From Trollope's Journal." *Partisan Review*, 28 (November 1961), 602. QT, CP / S.
9   wandered,]   ~ˌCP
10   floundered,]   ~ˌCP
16   uncultivated,]   ~ˌCP
Note: a typescript titled "Trollope in Washington" is in Houghton Library.

C126   "A Norther—Key West." *New Yorker*, 37 (Jan. 20, 1962), 25.

C127   "A Sentimental Tribute" (article). *Bryn Mawr Alumnae Bulletin*, 43 (Spring 1962), 2–3.

C128   "First Death in Nova Scotia." *New Yorker*, 38 (March 10, 1962), 36. QT, CP / S.

C129   "Sandpiper." *New Yorker*, 38 (July 21, 1962), 30. **B**22, QT, CP / S.
10   ocean]   Atlantic QT⁺
13   The world is marvellously]   And then the world is QT⁺
20   and mixed]   mixed QT⁺

C130   "From *The Death and Life of a Severino*" (tr. of João Cabral de Melo Neto). *Poetry*, 103 (October/November 1963), 10–18. CP, An.
printed with "A Note on the Poet" *signed* "E.B."]   *printed without note* CP⁺

C131   "Twelfth Morning; or What You Will." *New York Review of Books*, 2 (April 2, 1964), 5. QT, CP / S.
25   little.]   bit. QT⁺
25   a gallon]   the four-gallon QT⁺
unsigned]   *signed*: "Cabo Frio" QT⁺

C132   "The Smallest Woman in the World" (story; tr. of Clarice

Lispector). *Kenyon Review*, 26 (Summer 1964), 500–506. **B26**.

C133 "A Hen" (story; tr. of Clarice Lispector). *Kenyon Review*, 26 (Summer 1964), 507–509.

C134 "Marmosets" (story; tr. of Clarice Lispector). *Kenyon Review*, 26 (Summer 1964), 509–511. **B26**.

C135 "Flannery O'Connor, 1925–1964" (article). *New York Review of Books*, 3 (Oct. 8, 1964), 21. Reprinted as "Elizabeth Bishop: Poet." *Esprit*, 8 (Winter 1964), 14.

C136 "The Burglar of Babylon." *New Yorker*, 40 (Nov. 21, 1964), 56–57, QT, **A8**, CP / S.

　　fn. *one extra line of explication*: According to some, Micuçú is short for *mico sujo* (dirty marmoset).] *line omitted (explained in the introduction of* **A8***).* QT, CP

C137 "Seven-Sided Poem" (tr. of Carlos Drummond de Andrade). *Shenandoah*, 16 (Spring 1965), 5–6. CP, An.
printed with a footnote explaining her translation of "Universe, vast Universe"] *printed without explanation* CP+

C138 "Don't Kill Yourself" (tr. of Carlos Drummond de Andrade). *Shenandoah*, 16 (Spring 1965), 6–7. CP, An.
　20   for better]   for a better CP+
　22   wherefore]   wherefor An
　28   no,]   no∧An

C139 "On the Railroad Named Delight" (article). *New York Times Magazine*, March 7, 1965, pp. 30–31, 84–86. Sambas in this article reprinted with an unsigned note by EB as "Sambas." *Ploughshares*, 2, no. 4 (1975), 171.
printed in italics]   *roman   Ploughshares*
　10 arrived!]   ~. *Ploughshares*
　11 again!]   ~. *Ploughshares*
　20   Delight,]   ~∧*Ploughshares*
　23   Marshál]   Oh, ~ *Ploughshares*
　25   back.]   back! *Ploughshares*
printed with one footnote]   *printed with two footnotes, one new and one expanded   Ploughshares*

C140 "Travelling in the Family" (tr. of Carlos Drummond de Andrade). *Poetry*, 106 (June 1965), 181–184. CP, An.

C141 "Under the Window: Ouro Preto (for Lilli Correia de Araújo)." *New Yorker*, 42 (Dec. 24, 1966), 34. CP.
　34   I AM]   AM I CP
　46   How talkative are the seven ages of man]   The seven ages of

man are talkative CP

47   how . . . thirsty!] and . . .~~. CP

C142   "Rainy Season: Sub-Tropics." *Kenyon Review*, 29 (November 1967), 665–670. CP.

Giant Snail:

35–36/24–25   partly frozen ice] slowly melting CP

C143   "Going to the Bakery (Rio de Janeiro)." *New Yorker*, 44 (March 23, 1968), 40. CP.

13   compulsiveness, are taking off,] magnetic instances, take off‸ CP

C144   "Trouvée." *New Yorker*, 44 (Aug. 10, 1968), 89. CP.

1   Oh] ~, CP

C145   "House Guest." *New Yorker*, 44 (Dec. 7, 1968), 58. CP.

C146   "The Table" (tr. of Carlos Drummond de Andrade). *New York Review of Books*, 12 (Jan. 16, 1969), 12. CP, An.

printed with an introduction signed "Elizabeth Bishop"] *no introduction* CP+

23   Yes. Your] Yes, your An

153   rage,] ~‸An

203   discover] smoke out An

204   as well as those that] nor do I have those CP+

219   his useless son] just because of being useless CP+

220   *no such line*] may turn out to be, at least, CP+

220/221   to be] not CP+

222/223   stop,] ~; CP+

288/289   now)‸] ~), CP+

311/312   and with the thought, she did] her thought became her deed An

C147   "Thank-You Note." *Harvard Advocate*, 103 (Spring 1969), 20. Reprinted in *Antaeus*, 8(Winter 1973), 22.

C148   "In the Waiting Room." *New Yorker*, 47 (July 17, 1971), 34. B27, GIII.

17   The] the GIII

C149   "Crusoe in England." *New Yorker*, 47 (Nov. 6, 1971), 48. Reprinted in *Agenda*, 14 (Winter-Spring 1976), 25–30. GIII.

122   perpendicular] horizontal GIII

C150   "Cemetery of Childhood" (tr. of Joaquim Cardozo). *New Yorker*, 47 (Nov. 27, 1971), 52. An.

undated] *dated: Children's Week, 1953* An

12   afterglow] after-glow An

21   roadsides—]   ~: An
31   ground,]   ~; An
33, 39   Oh,]   ~! An
40   light!]   light. An
45   ransom,]   ~ˌAn

C151   "Sonnet of Intimacy" (tr. of Vinícius de Moraes). *New Yorker*, 47 (Nov. 27, 1971), 52. An.
5   riverbed]   river-bed An
10   unenviously.]   ~ˌAn
11   hiss,]   ~ˌAn

C152   "La Llave de Agua / The Key of Water" (tr. of Octavio Paz, by EB and the author). *Harvard Advocate*, 106 (Summer 1972), 14.

C153   "Por la Calle de Galeana / Along Galeana Street" (tr. of Octavio Paz, by EB and the author). *Harvard Advocate*, 106 (Summer 1972), 14.

C154   "La Arboleda / The Grove" (tr. of Octavio Paz, by EB and the author). *Harvard Advocate*, 106 (Summer 1972), 15.

C155   "The Moose." *New Yorker*, 48 (July 15, 1972), 27. Reprinted, and subtitled "The 1972 Phi Beta Kappa Poem," in *Harvard Magazine*, September 1972, p. 27. GIII.
15   Red Sea]   red sea GIII
40   is deepening]   grows richer GIII
50   to wet]   to their wet GIII
76   It's a]   A GIII
77   Boston,]   ~. GIII
78   regarding]   She regards GIII
87   divigation]   divagation GIII
104   re-married]   remarried GIII
118   half-groan, half-acceptance]   half groan, half acceptance GIII
159   R's]   r's GIII

C156   "Night City (from a Plane)." *New Yorker*, 48 (Sept. 16, 1972), 122. GIII.
(FROM A PLANE)]   FROM THE PLANE GIII

C157   "Poem (About the size of an old-style dollar bill)." *New Yorker*, 48 (Nov. 11, 1972), 46. Reprinted in *Agenda*, 14 (Winter-Spring 1976), 30–31. A11, GIII.

C158   "12 O'Clock News." *New Yorker*, 49 (March 24, 1973), 37. GIII.

C159   "A Brief Reminiscence and a Brief Tribute" (article). *Harvard Advocate: W. H. Auden, 1907–1973*, 108 [1974], 47–48.

C160 "Five Flights Up." *New Yorker*, 50 (Feb. 25, 1974), 40. GIII.

C161 "Objects and Apparitions (for Joseph Cornell)" (tr. of Octavio Paz). *New Yorker*, 50 (June 24, 1974), 32. **B28**, GIII.

  1 Hexagons] Hexahedrons GIII

C162 "Primero de Enero / January First" (tr. of Octavio Paz). *Ploughshares*, 2, no. 4 (1975), 14.

C163 "The End of March, Duxbury (for John Malcolm Brinnin and Bill Read) [The End of March]." *New Yorker*, 51 (March 24, 1975), 40. GIII.

The End of March, Duxbury] The End of March GIII

(For John Malcolm Brinnin and Bill Read] ˍ~ ~ ~ ~ ~ ~ Read: Duxburyˍ GIII

  55 dim, occasional] drab, damp, scattered GIII

  56 all of different colors] multi-colored GIII

  57 with . . . throwing . . . shadowsˍ] and . . . threw . . . ~, GIII

  58 and, after a minute, pulling] individual shadows, then pulled GIII

C164 "One Art." *New Yorker*, 52 (April 26, 1976), 40. GIII, **A14**, **A15**.

C165 "Memories of Uncle Neddy" (story). *Southern Review*, 13 (Fall 1977), 786–803.

C166 "Laureate's Words of Acceptance" (speech). *World Literature Today*, 51 (Winter 1977), 12. **H1**.

C167 "Santarém." *New Yorker*, 54 (Feb. 20, 1978), 40.

C168 "North Haven (In Memoriam: Robert Lowell)." *New Yorker*, 54 (Dec. 11, 1978), 40. **A16**. Reprinted in *Harvard Advocate*, 113 (November 1979), 25.

  4 *skin;*] ~, **A16**

  5 *carded*ˍ*horse's tail*] *carded, horse's-tail* **A16**

  7 have–] have **A16**

  8 drifting] —drifting **A16**

  9 south,] ~ˍ **A16**

  9 sidewise–] ~, **A16**

  11 month] ~, **A16**

  12 buttercups, red clover, purple vetch] Buttercups, Red Clover, Purple Vetch **A16**

  13 hawkweed . . . daisies . . . eyebright] Hawkweed . . . Daisies . . . Eyebright **A16**

  14 fragrant bedstraw's] Fragrant Bedstraw's **A16**

  16 goldfinches] Goldfinches **A16**

17 white-throated sparrow's] White-throated Sparrow's **A**16
24 fun,"] ~", **A**16
28 rearrange] re-arrange **A**16
C169 "Pink Dog." *New Yorker*, 55 (Feb. 26, 1979), 32.
C170 "Sonnet (Caught—the bubble)." *New Yorker*, 55 (Oct. 29, 1979), 38.

D

Translations

Dutch

Mimeographed Sheets

D1 Herzberg, Judith. *Elisabeth Bishop*. Rotterdam: Poetry International, 1976. 25 pp.
Contains the original followed by the Dutch translation: "Cirque d'Hiver" / "Cirque d'Hiver," pp. 1–2; "Manuelzinho" / "Manuelzinho," pp. 3–8; "Crusoe in England" / "Crusoe in Engeland," pp. 9–16; "Poem" / "Oedicut," pp. 17–20; "Visits to St. Elizabeths 1950" / "Bezoeken aan St. Elizabeth. 1950," pp. 21–24.

Anthology

D2 Bernlef, J. *Het ontplofte gedicht* Over poëzie. Amsterdam: Em. Querido's Uitgeverij B.V., 1978.
Contains "Eerstgestorvene in Nova Scotia" ("First Death in Nova Scotia"), pp. 79–80; "Pompstation" ("Filling Station"), pp. 81–82; "Een wonder als ontbijt" ("A Miracle for Breakfast"), pp. 82–83.

Book

D3 *Brazilië*. Amsterdam: Parool, 1963. 169 pp., tr. G. C. Mohr-Horsman.

French

Anthology

D4 Bosquet, Alain. *Trente-Cinq Jeunes Poètes Américains*. Paris: Nrf, Gallimard, 1960.

Contains (on facing pages) "A Summer's Dream" / "Un Rêve d'été," pp. 130–131; "Little Exercise" / "Petite exercice," pp. 134–135.

German

Periodical

D5 *Ensemble 7* (annual), *Internationales Jahrbuch für Literatur*, October 1976, pp. 154–155.
Contains (on facing pages) "The Imaginary Iceberg" / "Der imaginäre Eisberg," tr. Richard Exner.

Book

D6 *Brazilien.* Frankfurt: Internationale Presse, 1969. 159 pp., tr. Hans-Harald Herrmann.

Hebrew

Book

D7 *Brazil.* Tel Aviv: Sifriat, 1970. 156 pp., tr. Elchanan Kramer.

Italian

Anthology

D8 Izzo, Carlo. *Poesia americana del '900.* Guanda, 1963.
Contains (on facing pages) "A Miracle for Breakfast" / "Un miracolo per colazione," pp. 540–543; "The Unbeliever" / "Il miscredente," pp. 544–547.

Periodicals

D9 *Nuova corriente: rivistas di letteratura,* 5–6 (1956), 28–33.
Contains (on facing pages) "Visits to St. Elizabeth's" / "Visite all'Ospedale di Santa Elisabetta."

D10 *Inventario* (Florence, Milan), 17 (May-December 1962), 136–145.

Contains (on facing pages) "Il Monumento" / "The Monument," pp. 136/137–140/141; "Carta Geografica" / "The Map," pp. 140/141–142/143; "L'Armadillo—Brasile" / "The Armadillo—Brazil", pp. 142/143–144/145, tr. D. M. Pettinella.

D11 *Il sestante letterario* (Padua), 4 (January-February [and] March-April 1965), 27–28.
Contains "L'iceberg immaginario" ("The Imaginary Iceberg"), tr. D. M. Pettinella.

Latvian

Periodical

D12 *Jauna Gaita—112*, 22, no. 1(1977), 35–37.
Contains "Zivs" ("The Fish"), "Matu Mazgāšana" ("The Shampoo") and "Jau Tajumi Ceļojot" ("Questions of Travel"), tr. Astrīde Ivaska.

Portuguese

Periodicals

D13 *Cadernos brasileiros*, 6, no. 6 (November-December 1964), 61–67.
Contains (on facing pages) "The Burglar of Babylon" / "O Ladrão da Babilônia," tr. Flávio Macedo Soares.

D14 *Visão* (São Paulo), 35 (August 1, 1969), 51.
Contains "Debaixo da Janela: Ouro Prêto" ("Under the Window: Ouro Preto"), tr. Lili Corrêa de Araújo.

Spanish

Anthology

D15 Paz, Octavio. *Versiones y diversiones*. Mexico: Joaquín Mortiz, 1974.

Contains "El monumento" ("The Monument"), pp. 90–92; "Sueño de verano" ("A Summer's Dream"), pp. 92–93; "Visitas a St. Elizabeth" ("Visits to St. Elizabeth's"), pp. 93–96.

Periodical

D16 *Plural 19*, 19 (April 1973), 19.
Contains "Visita a St. Elizabeth" ("Visits to St. Elizabeths"), tr. Octavio Paz.

Book

D17 Elizabeth Bishop and the editors of *Life en Español. Brasil.* Edited for multicolor offset, South America. Calzada de la Viga No. 1332, Mexico, D.F., 1962. 160 pp.

E

Phonorecordings

E1 Harvard: Lamont Library (Poetry Room). *Selections from Her Poetry Read by the Author.* Not copyrighted. 78 RPM. December 17, 1947.
Contains "Songs for a Colored Singer," "Late Air," "The Fish," and "The Imaginary Iceberg."
This recording cannot be duplicated.

E2 Library of Congress. *Twentieth Century Poetry in English.* P-8 (P-38). Contains "Faustina, or Rock Roses," "Jerónimo's House," and "At the Fishhouses."
This recording was made in 1948 and issued in 1951. The Bishop recordings were reissued in 1954 on a 78 recording PL-9. PL-9, a 33⅓ RPM, is now available for $7.00 from The Recorded Sound Section, Music Division, Library of Congress 20540.

E3 *Pleasure Dome: An Audible Anthology of Modern Poetry Read by Its Creators and Edited by Lloyd Frankenberg.* Columbia Records (ML-4259), New York, 1949.
Contains "Anaphora," "Late Air," and "The Fish."
Released December 5, 1949. Often reissued from new matrixes; the earliest pressing has a dark blue label lettered in metallic yellowish white.

E4 [*Spoken Arts*] *Treasury of 100 Modern American Poets Reading Their Poems.* Spoken Arts SA 1049, vol. X.
Contains "The Imaginary Iceberg," "The Fish," "Varick Street," and "Visits to St. Elizabeths."
This recording was made in October 1968, in San Francisco. It is available at $6.98.

F

Musical Settings

F1 Rorem, Ned. "Visits to St. Elizabeths: (Bedlam)." For medium voice and piano; music by Ned Rorem; text by Elizabeth Bishop. Boosey and Hawkes, New York, 1964. Red and orange vertical stripes lettered in white; with a black and white drawing by Cocteau; six leaves. Recorded on: *Ned Rorem Songs*. Columbia MS 6561. Reissued on Odyssey 32 16 0274. Side 2, band 1. Soprano: Regina Sarfaty.

F2 Rorem, Ned. "Conversation." Music by Ned Rorem; poem by Elizabeth Bishop. Boosey and Hawkes, New York, 1969. Green with white horizontal stripes printed in black; two leaves.

F3 Carter, Elliott. "A Mirror on Which to Dwell." Sheet music not available. First performed at the Hunter College Playhouse on February 22, 1976, by Speculum Musicae and Susan Davenny-Wyner, soprano. Richard Fitz, conductor. Recorded May 11, 1977, by Columbia Records. Scheduled for release in late 1979; release postponed.

G

Book-Length Study of

Elizabeth Bishop

G1 Stevenson, Anne. *Elizabeth Bishop*. New York: Twayne Publishers, 1966. 144 pp. Abstract—CLC 1.

Contents: preface, p. [7]; acknowledgments, pp. [9–10]; introduction, pp. [11–13]; contents, p. [15]; chronology, p. 17; '1. The Traveler', p. 25; '2. The Artist', p. 51; '3. Precision and Resonance', p. 76; '4. Sources of Resonance: A View of Nature', p. 95; '5. The Ambiguity of Appearances', p. 107; '6. A Last Word', p. 126; 'A Note on Elizabeth Bishop's Critics', p. 128; 'Notes and References', p. 131; 'Selected Bibliography', p. 135; 'Index', p. 141.

Paper Issue: New Haven, Connecticut: College and University Press, Publishers, 1966.

Note: EB's father was William Thomas Bishop, not Thomas Bishop, p. 25.

H

Journal Issue Devoted to Elizabeth Bishop

H1   Ivask, Ivar, ed. "Homage to Elizabeth Bishop, Our 1976 Laureate." *World Literature Today*, 51 (Winter 1977), 4–52.

Contents:

Slater, Candace. "Brazil in the Poetry of Elizabeth Bishop," p. 33.

Taylor, Eleanor Ross. "Driving to the Interior: A Note on Elizabeth Bishop," p. 44.

Vendler, Helen. "Domestication, Domesticity, and the Otherworldly," p. 23.

I

Books Partially about

Elizabeth Bishop

I1   Frankenberg, Lloyd. "Elizabeth Bishop." *Pleasure Dome: On Reading Modern Poetry*. 1949; New York: Gordian Press, 1968, pp. 331–338.

I2   Frankenberg, Lloyd. "186. The Prodigal." *Invitation to Poetry: A Round of Poems from John Skelton to Dylan Thomas Arranged with Comments*. Garden City, N. Y.: Doubleday, 1956, p. 350.

I3   Guidacci, Margherita. *Studi su poeti e narratori Americani*. Saggi Letterari 4. Cagliari, Sardinia: Edes, Editrice Democratica Sarda, 1978, pp. 114–139. In Italian.

I4   Howard, Richard. "Comment." *Preferences*. New York: Viking Press, 1974, p. 31. **B27**.

I5   Jarrell, Randall. "Fifty Years of American Poetry." *The Third Book of Criticism*. New York: Farrar, Straus & Giroux, 1969, p. 325. Abstract—CLC 4. **J17**.

I6   Jarrell, Randall. "Poets." *Poetry and the Age*. New York: Alfred A. Knopf, 1953, pp. 223, 234–235. Abstract—CLC. **K1g**.

I7   Kalstone, David. "Elizabeth Bishop: Questions of Memory, Questions of Travel." *Five Temperaments: Elizabeth Bishop, Robert Lowell, James Merrill, Adrienne Rich, and John Ashbery*. New York: Oxford University Press, 1977, pp. 12–40.

I8   Malkoff, Karl. "Bishop, Elizabeth." *Crowell's Handbook of Contemporary American Poetry*. New York: Crowell, 1973, pp. 67–74.

I9   Mills, Ralph J., Jr. "Elizabeth Bishop." *Contemporary American Poetry*. New York: Random House, 1965, pp. 72–83. Abstract—ALLC.

I10   Moore, Marianne. "Archaically New." *Trial Balances*. Ed. Ann Winslow. New York: Macmillan, 1935, pp. 82–83. **B2**.

I11   Pinsky, Robert. *The Situation of Poetry: Contemporary Poetry and Its Traditions*. Princeton, N. J.: Princeton University Press, 1976, pp. 75–77, 162.

I12   Rizza, Peggy. "Another Side of This Life: Women as Poets." *American Poetry since 1960: Some Critical Perspectives*. Ed. Robert B. Shaw. London: Carcanet, 1973, pp. 167–171. Abstract—CLC 4.

I13   Rosenthal, M. L. *The Modern Poets*. New York: Oxford Press, 1960, pp. 253–255, 261.

I14   Stepanchev, Stephen. "Elizabeth Bishop." *American Poetry since 1945*. New York: Harper and Row, 1965, pp. 69–79. Abstract— CLC 4.

I15   True, Michael. *Worcester Poets, with Notes toward a Literary History*. Foreword by Stanley Kunitz. Worcester, Mass. The Worcester Poetry Association, 1972, pp. 35–36, 39, 41. Printed in an edition of five hundred, this book was first offered for sale November 19, 1972. It contains biographical information on Bishop and her family but repeats the Stevenson (**G1**) error, giving her father's name incorrectly.

I16   Unterecker, John E. "Elizabeth Bishop." *American Writers: A Collection of Literary Biographies*. Supplement I, part I. Ed. Leonard Ungar. New York: Charles Scribner's Sons, 1979, pp. 72–97. There is a two-page bibliography by Lloyd Schwartz.

J

Articles about Elizabeth Bishop and Her Work

J1 Anonymous. "Poets among Us." *Vogue*, 121 (April 15, 1953), 91.

J2 Bloom, Harold. "The Necessity of Misreading." *Georgia Review*, 29 (Summer 1975), 267.

J3 Brown, Ashley. "An Interview with Elizabeth Bishop." *Shenandoah*, 17 (Winter 1966), 3. Annotated—ATCL. **Q2.**

J4 Brown, Ashley. "Elizabeth Bishop in Brazil." *Southern Review*, 13 (Fall 1977), 688.

J5 Byatt, A. S. "Women Writers in America: A. S. Byatt Examines the Contribution of Women Writers to the American Literary Tradition and Sheila Hale Talks to Ten of the Most Important in America Today." *Harpers and Queen*, July 1978, pp. 59–61.

J6 Chittick, V. L. O. "Nominations for a Laureateship." *Dalhousie Review*, 35 (Summer 1955), 145.

J7 Eberhart, Richard. "The Muse—With Yankee Accent." *Saturday Review of Literature*, 32 (March 19, 1949), 9.

J8 Ehrenpreis, Irvin. "Viewpoint." *Times Literary Supplement*, Feb. 8, 1974, 132.

J9 Emig, Janet A. "The Poem as Puzzle." *English Journal*, 52 (1963), 222.

J10 Estess, Sybil. "Shelters for 'What Is Within': Meditation and Epiphany in the Poetry of Elizabeth Bishop." *Modern Poetry Studies*, 8 (Spring 1977), 50.

J11 Estess, Sybil. "Elizabeth Bishop: The Delicate Art of Map Making." *Southern Review*, 13 (Fall 1977), 705.

J12   Fowlie, Wallace. "Poetry of Silence." *Commonweal*, 65 (Feb. 15, 1957), 514. Abstract—ALLC; annotated—ATCL.

J13   Frankenberg, Lloyd. "Meaning in Modern Poetry." *Saturday Review of Literature*, 29 (March 23, 1946), 5.

J14   Fraser, G. S. "Some Younger American Poets." *Commentary*, 23 (May 1957), 461.

J15   Gordon, Jan B. "Days and Distances: The Cartographic Imagination of Elizabeth Bishop." *Salmagundi*, 22–23 (Spring/Summer 1973), 294. Collected in *Contemporary Poetry in America*, ed. Robert Boyers (New York: Shocken, 1974), p. 370.

J16   Hopkins, Crale D. "Inspiration as a Theme: Art and Nature in the Poetry of Elizabeth Bishop." *Arizona Quarterly*, 32 (Autumn 1976), 197.

J17   Jarrell, Randall. "Fifty Years of American Poetry." *Prairie Schooner*, 37 (Spring 1963), 1. I5.

J18   Kalstone, David. "Conjuring with Nature: Some Twentieth-Century Readings of the Pastoral." *Twentieth Century Literature in Retrospect*. Ed. Reuben Brower. Harvard English Studies 2. Cambridge, Mass.: Harvard University Press, 1971, p. 247.

J19   Kalstone, David. "Questions of Memory—New Poems by Elizabeth Bishop." *Ploughshares*, 2, no. 4 (1975), 173.

J20   McNally, Nancy L. "Elizabeth Bishop: The Discipline of Description." *Twentieth-Century Literature*, 11 (January 1966), 189. Contains checklist; annotated—ATCL.

J21   Mazzaro, Jerome. "Elizabeth Bishop and the Poetics of Impediment." *Salmagundi*, 27 (Summer/Fall 1974), 118.

J22   Moore, Richard. "Elizabeth Bishop: 'The Fish.' " *Boston University Studies in English*, 2 (1956), 251.

J23   Paz, Octavio. "Elizabeth Bishop o El Poder de la Retensia." *Plural*, 5 (October 1975), 6. Translated in H1.

J24   Schwartz, Lloyd. "One Art: The Poetry of Elizabeth Bishop, 1971–1976." *Ploughshares*, 3, nos. 3 and 4 (1977), 30.

J25   Shore, Jane. "Elizabeth Bishop: The Art of Changing Your Mind." *Ploughshares*, 5, no. 1 (1979), 178.

J26   Smith, William Jay. "Geographical Questions: The Recent Poetry of Elizabeth Bishop." *Hollins Critic*, 14 (February 1977), 2. K11cc.

J27   Southworth, James G. "The Poetry of Elizabeth Bishop." *College English*, 20 (February 1959), 213. Abstract—ALLC; annotated—ATCL.

J28   Spiegelman, Willard. "Landscape and Knowledge: The Poetry of Elizabeth Bishop." *Modern Poetry Studies*, 6 (Winter 1975), 203.

J29   Spiegelman, Willard. "Elizabeth Bishop's 'Natural Heroism.'" *Centennial Review*, 22, no. 1 (Winter 1978), 14.

J30   Starbuck, George. " 'The Work!' A Conversation with Elizabeth Bishop." *Ploughshares*, 3, nos. 3 and 4 (1977), 11. Q11.

J31   Stevenson, Anne. "The Poetry of Elizabeth Bishop: Precision and Resonance." *Shenandoah*, 17 (Winter 1966), 45. Annotated— ATCL. G1.

J32   Thompson, Karl F. " 'The Colder the Air.' " *Explicator*, 12 (March 1954), 33. Reprinted in *The Explicator Cyclopedia*, 1 (Chicago: Quadrangle Books, 1966), 18.

K

Reviews

K1   *North & South*

K1a   Anonymous. *Kirkus Reviews*, 14 (Aug. 1, 1946), 380. Abstract
—BRD 1946.

K1b   Anonymous. *United States Quarterly Book List*, 3 (March 1947),
21.

K1c   Bogan, Louise. "Verse." *New Yorker*, 22 (Oct. 5, 1946), 113.
Abstract—BRD 1946.

K1d   Brunsdale, Lucy. "Review and Comment." *Vassar Brew*, October 1946, p. 17.

K1e   Frankenberg, Lloyd. "A Meritorious Prize Winnter." *Saturday
Review of Literature*, 29 (Oct. 12, 1946), 46. Abstract—ALLC, BRD
1946.

K1f   Gibbs, Barbara. "A Just Vision." *Poetry*, 69 (January 1947), 228.
Abstract—BRD 1946.

K1g   Jarrell, Randall. "The Poet and His Public." *Partisan Review*, 13
(1946), 488. I6.

K1h   Lowell, Robert. "Thomas, Bishop, and Williams." *Sewanee Review*, 55 (Summer 1947), 497.

K1i   Mizener, Arthur. "New Verse." *Furioso*, 2 (Spring 1947), 72.

K1j   Moore, Marianne. "A Modest Expert." *Nation*, 163 (Sept. 28,
1946), 354.
Misquotes "Roosters," lines 82–83: Peter's | falling] NS; Peter's |
folly Moore.

K1k   Rodman, Selden. "Carefully Revealed." *New York Times Book
Review*, Oct. 27, 1946, p. 18.

K1l   Rosenthal, M. L. "In Poetic Perspective: Many Experiments in
Verse, Traditional and Experimental." *New York Herald Tribune
Weekly Book Review*, May 18, 1947, p. 2.

K1m Snell, George. *San Francisco Chronicle*, Jan. 12, 1947, p. 20.

K1n Weeks, Edward. "Prize Poet." *Atlantic*, 178 (August 1946), 148.

K1o Williams, Oscar. "North but South." *New Republic*, 115 (Oct. 21, 1946), 525. Abstract—BRD 1946.

K2   Poems: North & South—A Cold Spring

K2a Alvarez, A. "Imagism and Poetesses." *Kenyon Review*, 19 (Spring 1957), 321.

K2b Anonymous. *Kirkus Reviews*, 23 (May 1, 1955), 320. Abstract—BRD 1955.

K2c Anonymous. *United States Quarterly Book Review*, 11 (December 1955), 474.

K2d Bogan, Louise. "The Poet Dickinson Comes to Life." *New Yorker*, 31 (Oct. 8, 1955), 179.

K2e Booth, Philip. *Village Voice*, Jan. 25, 1956, p. 7.

K2f Eberhart, Richard. "With Images of Actuality." *New York Times Book Review*, July 17, 1955, p. 4.

K2g Honig, Edwin. "Poetry Chronicle." *Partisan Review*, 23 (Winter 1956), 115.

K2h Nemerov, Howard. "The Poems of Elizabeth Bishop." *Poetry*, 87 (December 1955), 179. Abstract—ALLC.

K2i Rosenberger, Coleman. *New York Herald Tribune Book Review*, Sept. 4, 1955, p. 2.

K3   Poems, 1956

K3a Anonymous. "In and Out of Line." *Times Literary Supplement*, Feb. 1, 1957, p. 66.

K3b Fraser, G. S. "Potential for Variety." *New Statesman*, 53 (Jan. 5, 1957), 22.

K4   The Diary of "Helena Morley"

K4a Adams, Mildred. "Yesterday's Girlhood." *New York Times Book Review*, Dec. 29, 1957, p. 5.

K4b   Anonymous. "General." *New Yorker*, 33 (Jan. 18, 1958), 97.

K4c   Benét, Rosemary Carr. "Young Brazilian Pepys." *Saturday Review of Literature*, 41 (Jan. 18, 1958), 58.

K4d   Goldensohn, Lorrie. *American Book Review*, 1 (October 1978), 10.

K4e   Moore, Marianne. "Imagination in Action." *Poetry*, 94 (July 1959), 247.
The last quotation is incorrectly attributed to Elizabeth Bishop, " 'that happiness does not. . . .' " It belongs to Mrs. Brant.

K4f   Reid, Alastair. "Immortal Diamond." *New Yorker*, 54 (May 29, 1978), 114.

K4g   Watson, Frances. *Listener*, Jan. 22, 1959, p. 179.

K5   *Brazil*

K5a   Sensabaugh, L. F. *Hispanic American Historical Review*, 43 (August 1963), 479.

K6   *Questions of Travel*

K6a   Anonymous. *Choice*, 2 (Feb. 1966), 858. Abstract—BRD 1966.

K6b   Anonymous. "The Passing Strange." *Time*, 86 (Dec. 24, 1965), 64.

K6c   Baro, Gene. "Clear Vision." *New York Times Book Review*, March 26, 1967, p. 5. Abstract—ALLC.

K6d   Booth, Philip. "The Poet as Voyager." *Christian Science Monitor*, 58 (Jan. 6, 1966), 10.

K6e   Davis, Douglas M. "The Measure of Prominent Poets: Views from Brazil and the Campus." *National Observer*, 4 (Dec. 27, 1965), 17.

K6f   Davison, Peter. "The Gilt Edge of Reputation." *Atlantic*, 217 (January 1966), 85.

K6g   Dickey, William. "The Thing Itself." *Hudson Review*, 19 (Spring 1966), 154.

K6h   Ehrenpreis, Irvin. "Solitude and Isolation." *Virginia Quarterly Review*, 42 (Spring 1966), 332.

K6i   Fields, Kenneth. "J. V. Cunningham and Others." *Southern Review*, 5 (Spring 1969), 568.

K6j Garrigue, Jean. "Elizabeth Bishop's School." *New Leader*, 48 (Dec. 6, 1965), 22.

K6k Hochman, Sandra. "Some of America's Most Natural Resources." *Book Week*, Feb. 20, 1966, p. 4.

K6l Martz, L. L. "Recent Poetry: Looking for a Home." *Yale Review*, 55 (Spring 1966), 458.

K6m Mazzocco, Robert. "A Poet of Landscape." *New York Review of Books*, 9 (Oct. 12, 1967), 4.

K6n Michelson, Peter. "Sentiment and Artifice: Elizabeth Bishop and Isabella Gardner." *Chicago Review*, 18, nos. 3 and 4 (1966), 188.

K6o Moss, Howard. "All Praise." *Kenyon Review*, 28 (March 1966), 255. Abstract—CLC 1.

K6p Mueller, Lisel. "The Sun the Other Way Around." *Poetry*, 108 (August 1966), 335. Abstract—ALLC.

K6q Nelson, E. *Library Journal*, 90 (Oct. 1, 1965), 4090. Abstract—BRD 1966.

K6r Pryce-Jones, Alan. "2 Contrasting Ways to Write Poetry Today." *New York Herald Tribune*, 125 (Jan. 1, 1966), 9.

K6s Smith, William J. "New Books of Poems." *Harper's*, 233 (August 1966), 89.

K6t Tomlinson, Charles. "Elizabeth Bishop's New Book." *Shenandoah*, 17 (Winter 1966), 88.

K6u Warnke, Frank J. "The Voyages of Elizabeth Bishop." *New Republic*, 154 (April 9, 1966), 19.

K7 *Selected Poems*

K7a Bernlef, J. "Judith Herzberg en Elizabeth Bishop." *Gids*, 131, no. 5:325. In Dutch.

K7b Dodsworth, Martin. "The Human Note." *Listener*, 78 (Nov. 30, 1967), 720.

K7c Dodsworth, Martin. "Unamerican Editions." *Times Literary Supplement*, Nov. 23, 1967, p. 1106. Began a correspondence published in "Letters to the Editor": December 7, 1967, a letter by Ian Parsons and a comment by Martin Dodsworth; January 18, 1968, two letters by I. Ehrenpreis and Martin Dodsworth; January 25, 1968, a letter by Ian Parsons; February 8, 1968, a letter by Elizabeth Bishop, R3.

K7d Grant, Damian. "Outlandish Poems." *Tablet*, Feb. 3, 1968, p. 108.

K7e Hamilton, Ian. "Women's-Eye Views." *Observer*, Dec. 31, 1967, p. 20.

K7f Hayman, R. "Books and Writers." *Encounter*, 31 (July 1968), 71.

K7g Jones, Brian. "Singling Out." *London Magazine*, 7 (March 1968), 84.

K7h Kavanagh, P. J. "Poetry and Manners." Manchester *Guardian Weekly*, 97 (Nov. 2, 1967), 11.

K8   *The Ballad of the Burglar of Babylon*

K8a Agree, R. H. *Instructor*, 78 (August/September 1968), 190.

K8b Bacon, Martha. "The Children's Trip to the Gallows." *Atlantic*, 222 (December 1968), 152.

K8c Dorsey, M. A. *Library Journal*, 93 (May 15, 1968), 2118. Abstract—BRD 1968.

K8d Maddocks, Melvin. "For Poets of All Ages." *Christian Science Monitor*, 60 (May 2, 1968), B9.

K8e Rexroth, Kenneth. "Song of a Hunted Man." *New York Times Book Review*, Pt. 2 (May 5, 1968), p. 2.

K8f Scanlon, L. P. "Briefly Noted and Late Arrivals." *Commonweal*, 89 (Nov. 22, 1968), 294.

K9   *The Complete Poems*

K9a Adams, Phoebe. 20 words in *Atlantic*, 223 (May 1969), 112.

K9b Anonymous. *Choice*, 6 (September 1969), 812. Abstract—BRD 1969.

K9c Anonymous. "Notes on Current Books." *Virginia Quarterly Review*, 45 (Autumn 1969), cxxxii. Abstract—CLC 4.

K9d Arnold, Walter E. "Critics' Choices for Christmas." *Commonweal*, 91 (Dec. 5, 1969), 311.

K9e Ashbery, John. "The Complete Poems: Throughout Is This Quality of Thingness." *New York Times Book Review*, June 1, 1969, p. 8.

K9f Brownjohn, Alan. "Absorbing Chaos." *New Statesman*, 80 (Dec. 4, 1970), 772.

K9g Burns, Gerald. "Our Common Reader Attacks the Greats." *Southwest Review*, 54 (Summer 1969), 335.

K9h Cluysenaar, Anne. "New and Translated Poetry." *Stand*, 12, no. 3 (1971), 72.

K9i Constable, John. "John Constable on the Poetry of Elizabeth Bishop." *Spectator*, 227 (Sept. 18, 1971), 416.

K9j Cotter, James F. "Does Poetry Have an Audience?" *America*, 122 (Feb. 21, 1970), 187.

K9k Dodsworth, Martin. "America Observed." Manchester *Guardian Weekly*, 103 (Dec. 19, 1970), 20.

K9l Dunn, Douglas. "Snatching the Bays." *Encounter*, 36 (March 1971), 67.

K9m [Ehrenpreis, Irvin.] "Loitering between Dream and Experience." *Times Literary Supplement*, Jan. 22, 1971, p. 92.

K9n Elliott, Charles. "A Minor Poet with a Major Fund of Love." *Life*, 67 (July 4, 1969), 13.

K9o Ewart, Gavin. "Voices from Overseas." *Ambit*, 47 (1971), 34.

K9p Fuller, John, "The Iceberg and the Ship." *Listener*, 85 (April 8, 1971), 456.

K9q Harrison, Tony. "Wonderland." *London Magazine*, 11 (April/ May 1971), 163.

K9r Hughes, Daniel. "American Poetry 1969: From B-Z." *Massachusetts Review*, 11 (Autumn 1970), 679.

K9s Jaffe, Don. "Voice of the Poet: Oracular, Eerie, Daring." *Saturday Review of Literature*, 52 (Sept. 6, 1969), 29.

K9t James, Clive. "Everything's Rainbow." *Review*, 25 (Spring 1971), 51.

K9u Kalstone, David. "All Eye." *Partisan Review*, 37 (Spring 1970), 310.

K9v Kirby-Smith, H. T., Jr. "Miss Bishop and Others." *Sewanee Review*, 80 (Summer 1972), 483. Abstract—CLC 4.

K9w Lask, T. "The Window and the Mirror." *New York Times*, June 7, 1969, p. 37.

K9x Mazzaro, Jerome. "Elizabeth Bishop's Poems." *Shenandoah*, 20 (Summer 1969), 99.

K9y Nelson, E. R. *Library Journal*, 94 (May 1, 1969), 1883. Abstract—BRD 1969.

K9z Nelson, Elizabeth. *Spirit*, 36 (Summer 1969), 37.

K9aa Porter, Peter. "Dazzling Landscapes." *Observer Review*, Jan. 3, 1971, p. 30.

K9bb Sheehan, Donald. "The Silver Sensibility: Five Recent Books of American Poetry." *Contemporary Literature*, 12 (Winter 1971), 98.

K9cc Stanford, Derek. "Transatlantic Rimbaud." *Books and Bookmen*, 16 (January 1971), 36.

K9dd Taylor, Henry. "A Gathering of Poets." *Western Humanities Review*, 23 (Autumn 1969), 366.

K9ee Walsh, Chad. "Never Underestimate the Power of a Lady's Voice." *Book World*, April 27, 1969, p. 8. Abstract—BRD 1969.

K10 *An Anthology of Twentieth-Century Brazilian Poetry*

K10a Aguilar, Helene Farber de. "Poetry from Latin America: 'The Most Important Harvest of the Times.' " *Parnassus: Poetry in Review*, 1 (Spring/Summer 1973), 175. *PN 1010 . P3*

K10b Anonymous. *Choice*, 9 (Nov. 1972), 1136. Abstract—BRD 1972. *u . L .*

K10c Gant, Liz. "An Anthology of 20th Century Brazilian Poetry." *Black World*, 22 (June 1973), 92. *E 185. 5 . N 3 815   2 also micro*

K10d Neiswender, Rosemary. *Library Journal*, 97 (July 1972), 2404. *Libr. Sci.*

K10e Sayers, Raymond. *Modern Language Journal*, 57 (April 1973), 232. *PB 1 . M47*

K10f Schramm, Richard. "A Gathering of Poets." *Western Humanities Review*, 26 (Autumn 1972), 398. *AP2 . W 426*

K10g Vendler, Helen. *New York Times Book Review*, Jan. 7, 1973, p. 4. *u . L . —   also micro.*

K11 *Geography III*

K11a Bloom, Harold. "Books Considered." *New Republic*, 176 (Feb. 5, 1977), 29.

K11b Bromwich, David. "Verse Chronicle." *Hudson Review*, 30 (Summer 1977), 279.

K11c Corn, Alfred. *Georgia Review*, 31 (Summer 1977), 533.

K11d Estess, Sybil P. "The Delicate Art of Map Making." *Southern Review*, 13 (Fall 1977), 705.

K11e Goldensohn, Lorrie. "Elizabeth Bishop's Originality." *American Poetry Review*, 7 (March/April 1978), 18.

K11f Graves, Steven. "A Gifted Poet Writes of Life." *Deseret News*, Aug. 24, 1977, p. C13.

K11g Gray, Paul. "A Quartet of Poets Singing Solo." *Time*, 109 (March 22, 1977), 90.

K11h Hecht, Anthony. "Awful but Cheerful." *Times Literary Supplement*, Aug. 26, 1977, p. 1024.

K11i Hollander, John. "Questions of Geography." *Parnassus: Poetry in Review*, 5 (Spring/Summer 1977), 359.

K11j Howes, Victor. " 'Geography III' Focuses on Place." *Christian Science Monitor*, 69 (Feb. 9, 1977), 27.

K11k Jefferson, Margo. "The Map Maker." *Newsweek*, 89 (Jan. 31, 1977), 73.

K11l Jones, Robert C. "The Poems, Though So Few, Are Worthy of an Award." *Kansas City Star*, Feb. 6, 1977, p. 10D.

K11m Jones, S. Jeffrey. " 'Geography III' Deserves Wide Audience." *News & Courier / Charleston Evening Post*, April 3, 1977, p. 4-E.

K11n Lask, Thomas. "Serene and Star-crazed." *New York Times*, Jan. 22, 1977, p. 19.

K11o Lask, Thomas. "Serenity in a New Country, Stridency in the Stars." *Chicago Tribune*, Feb. 6, 1977, Section 7, p. 4.

K11p Leibowitz, Herbert. "Geography III: The Elegant Maps of Elizabeth Bishop." *New York Times Book Review*, Feb. 6, 1977, p. 7.

K11q Magrinat, Gustav. "Old Haunts and New Ground for Bishop." *Greensboro Daily News*, Aug. 14, 1977, p. D3.

K11r McClatchy, J. D. "The Other Bishop." *Canto*, 1 (Winter 1977), 165.

K11s McPherson, William. "The Famous Eye." *Washington Post Book World*, Feb. 6, 1977, p. F7.

K11t McPherson, William. "The Literary Scene." *New York Post*, 176 (Feb. 10, 1977), 15.

K11u Middleton, Harry. "Odds and Ends." *Figaro*, April 6, 1977, 17.

K11v Mullen, Richard F. *America*, 136 (June 18, 1977), 552.

K11w North, Charles. "Abstraction and Elizabeth Bishop." St. Mark's Church *Poetry Project Newsletter*, 48 (Oct. 1, 1977), 5.

K11x Porter, Peter. "What's Become of Browning?" London *Observer*, Oct. 2, 1977, p. 26.

K11y Reid, Christopher. "Bishop's Benedictions." *New Review*, 4, no. 43 (October 1977), 50.

K11z Robb, Christina. "Where Has This Poet Gone Alone?" *Boston Globe*, Jan. 14, 1977, p. 32.

K11aa Schwartz, Lloyd. "How Little, but How Rich Is This Reward in Poetry." *Boston Herald American*, Jan. 23, 1977, p. A–26.

K11bb   Seymour-Smith, Martin. "Some American Styles." Edinburgh *Weekend Scotsman*, Nov. 14, 1970, p. 3.

K11cc   Smith, William Jay. "Geographical Questions: The Recent Poetry of Elizabeth Bishop." *Hollins Critic*, 14, no. 1 (February 1977), 1. **J26**.

K11dd   Talmey, Allene. "Books." *Vogue*, 168 (August 1978), 42.

K11ee   Vendler, Helen. "Recent Poetry: Eight Poets." *Yale Review*, 66 (Spring 1977), 407.

K11ff   Vukelich, George. "Bishop's Poetry: Precision, Simplicity." Madison, Wis. *Capital Times*, Jan. 17, 1977, p. 14.

K11gg   Wood, Michael. "RSVP." *New York Review of Books*, 24 (June 9, 1977), 29.

K12   Music Reviews: "A Mirror on Which to Dwell"

K12a   Henahan, Donal. "Carter's 'A Mirror' Given Premiere by a New Group." *New York Times*, Feb. 26, 1976, p. 22.

K12b   Porter, Andrew. "Reflections." *New Yorker*, 52 (March 8, 1976), 122.

K12c   Schiff, David. "Elliott Carter: A Mirror on Which to Dwell." *New York Arts Journal*, 2 (Spring 1977), 41.

K12d   Schwartz, Lloyd. " 'Words and Music' Eloquent yet Casual." *Boston Herald American*, May 11, 1977, p. 30.

L

Current Biography

(For the most detailed biographies, see **G1**, **H1**, and *Current Biography*.)

L1   *Celebrity Register,* 3d ed. (1973), p. 47.

L2   *Contemporary Authors,* condensed vols. 5–8, first revision (1969), pp. 112–114.

L3   *Current Biography,* 38 (September 1977), 15–17.

L4   *Current Biography Yearbook 1977,* 38 (1977–78), 60–62.

L5   *International Who's Who,* 38th ed. (1974–75), p. 164.

L6   *Who's Who in America,* 39th ed. 1 (A-K) (1976–77), 283.

L7   *Who's Who in the East,* 14th ed. (1974–75), p. 63.

L8   *Who's Who of American Women,* 8th ed. (1974–75), p. 80.

M

Notices of Awards

M1 "Books—Authors." *New York Times*, July 5, 1945, p. 11.
Announcement of the Houghton Mifflin Award.

M2 "Poetry Society Awards Shelley Memorial Prize." *New York Times*, Jan. 6, 1953, p. 8.

M3 "Five Are Elected to Arts Institute." *New York Times*, Feb. 10, 1954, p. 36.
Bishop is elected to Lifetime Membership in the National Institute of Arts and Letters.

M4 "Franklin's Ideals Seen Lost Today: R. E. Sherwood Notes Trend toward Suspicion—Academy of Arts Makes Awards." *New York Times*, May 27, 1954, p. 5.
Bishop is inducted into membership in the National Institute of Arts and Letters.

M5 " 'Anne Frank' Pulitzer Play, 'Andersonville' Prize Novel." *New York Times*, May 8, 1956, p. 1.
Pulitzer Prize for *Poems: North & South—Cold Spring*.

M6 "Sketches of the Pulitzer Prize Winners for 1956 in Journalism, Letters, and Music." *New York Times*, May 8, 1956, p. 24.
A brief biographical description.

M7 "The Pulitzer Awards." *New York Times*, May 8, 1956, p. 32.
Pulitzer Prize for *Poems: North and South—A Cold Spring*.

M8 "Elizabeth Bishop Wins '64 Poetry Fellowship." *New York Times*, Sept. 30, 1964, p. 40.
1964 Fellowship of the Academy of American Poets.

M9 Henry Raymont. "Winners of the 1969 Book Awards Named." *New York Times*, March 3, 1970, p. 34.
National Book Award for *The Complete Poems*.

M10 Henry Raymont. "Criticism Mounts over Book Awards Procedure." *New York Times*, March 5, 1970, p. 36.

Lowell accepted for Bishop. He read "Visits to St. Elizabeths" to protest Pound's never having received the award. This caused Kenneth Rexroth to jump to his feet, calling Lowell "an anti-Semitic fascist."

M11 "Prize to Elizabeth Bishop." *New York Times*, Feb. 21, 1976, p. 16.
In a filler at the bottom of the page, the paper announces that Bishop has won the Neustadt Award.

M12 "Books Abroad Choice Called Surprise." *Norman* (Oklahoma) *Transcript*, Feb. 22, 1976, p. 2.
Neustadt Award.

M13 Joyce Illig. "Book Business." *Washington Post Book World*, Feb. 29, 1976, p. F6.
Neustadt Award.

M14 "Notes on People." *New York Times*, Dec. 4, 1976, p. 30.
Bishop is elected to the American Academy of Arts and Letters.

M15 "Book Critics Circle Announces Prizes in Four Categories." *New York Times*, Jan. 7, 1977, p. B2.
National Book Critics Circle Award for *Geography III*.

M16 Eliot Fremont-Smith. "Making Book." *Village Voice*, Jan. 17, 1977, p. 81.
An announcement of the NBCC awards.

M17 "An Award Rediscovers." *Kansas City Star*, Feb. 6, 1977, p. 10D.
NBCC Award.

M18 "News Notes." *Poetry*, 130 (April 1977), 56.
NBCC Award.

M19 Joseph F. Sullivan. "Princeton Confers 1,589 Degrees on Its 232d Commencement Day." *New York Times*, June 13, 1979, B7.
Doctor of Letters from Princeton.

N

Works Which Mention
Elizabeth Bishop

N1 Allen, Walter. "English Poets: [A review of] *The Chatto Book of Modern Poetry, 1915–1955.*" *New Statesman*, 52 (July 14, 1956), 47–48.

N2 Alvarez, A. "Robert Lowell in Conversation." *Profile of Robert Lowell.* Comp. Jerome Mazzaro. Columbus, Ohio: Merrill, 1971, p. 37.

N3 Andrade, Carlos Drummond de. "A Writer Is Born and Dies." Tr. Ricardo da Silveira Lobo Sternberg. *Ploughshares*, 2, no. 4 (1975), 241.
Acknowledgment is made to EB for her help with the translation.

N4 Anonymous. "Poets: The Second Chance." *Time*, 89 (June 2, 1967), 68.

N5 Austin, Louise Paye, editor-in-chief. *Vassarion*, 1932, (Poughkeepsie, N. Y., 1934), 147.
Vassar College Choir, second soprano.

N6 Berryman, John. *The Freedom of the Poet.* New York: Farrar, Straus and Giroux, 1976, pp. 298–99, 317.

N7 Bloom, Harold. "Harold Bloom on Poetry." *New Republic*, 173 (Nov. 29, 1975), 26.
Bloom says that Miss Bishop is one of our two best living poets.

N8 Bogan, Louise. *Achievement in American Poetry, 1900–1950.* Chicago: Henry Regnery, 1951, pp. 105, 139.
Bogan mentions Bishop as a younger writer of the forties, comparing her poetry with that of Marianne Moore.

N9 Brown, Ashley. "An Interview with James Merrill." *Shenandoah*, 19 (Summer 1968), 7, 11, 12.

Merrill mentions Bishop's "The Riverman." Brown mentions her twice in comparisons.

N10   Charlton, Linda. "Poet Prizes to Lowell and Strand." *New York Times*, April 11, 1974, p. 28.

Bishop is one of the judges for the Copernicus Award and the Edgar Allen Poe Award.

N11   Cole, William. "Trade Winds: Academia Nuts." *Saturday Review*, 4 (Feb. 19, 1977), 36.

Cole mentions the people he saw going to the Bishop meeting at MLA: Mark Strand, James Merrill, William Meredith, Howard Moss, Heather McHugh, Terry Stokes, and Rachel Hadas.

N12   Frankenberg, Lloyd. "The Poets: Their Spoken Words Attract a New Audience." *Harper's Bazaar*, August 1950, p. 139.

N13   Hall, Donald. "The Art of Poetry IV—Marianne Moore" (interview). *Paris Review*, 7, no. 26 (1961), 51.

N14   Lowell, Robert. "On 'Skunk Hour.' " *The Contemporary Poet as Artist and Critic*. Ed. Anthony Ostroff. Boston: Little Brown, 1964, p. 109.

N15   McClatchy, J. D. "Robert Lowell: Learning to Live in History." *American Poetry Review*, 6 (January/February 1977), 34.

N16   Moore, Marianne. *A Marianne Moore Reader*. New York: Viking Press, 1961, pp. 226–229, 237, 260.

N17   Moss, Howard. "Books: The Poet's Voice" (Review of *Five Temperaments*). *New Yorker*, 53 (Feb. 13, 1978), 118–124.

N18   Oates, Joyce Carol. "Joyce Carol Oates on Poetry." *New Republic*, 179 (Dec. 9, 1978), 25.

N19   O'Brien, Edward J. *The Best Short Stories 1938 and the Yearbook of the American Short Story*. Boston and New York: Houghton Mifflin, 1938, p. 393.

"The Baptism" is listed on the "Honor Roll" of *The Yearbook* and is given a three-star rating.

N20   Rabell, Caroline Alice, editor-in-chief. *The 1933 Vassarion*, 44 (Poughkeepsie, N. Y., 1934), 115, 117, 120.

Vassar Miscellany News, p. 115, first one, second row; *Vassarion*, p. 117, junior editor, last one, second row; *Vassar College Choir*, p. 120, second soprano.

N21   Rexroth, Kenneth. *American Poetry in the Twentieth Century*. New York: Herder and Herder, 1971, p. 125.

N22   Rorem, Ned. *Critical Affairs: A Composer's Journal*. New York: Braziller, 1970, pp. 28–29.

N23 Seidel, Frederick. "The Art of Poetry III—Robert Lowell" (interview). *Paris Review*, 7, no. 26 (1961), 69.

N24 Sexton, Anne. *Anne Sexton: A Self-Portrait in Letters*. Ed. Linda Gray Sexton and Lois Ames. Boston: Houghton Mifflin, 1977, pp. 94, 146, 376.

N25 Strand, Mark. "A Conversation [with Norman Klein]." *Ploughshares*, 2, no. 3 (1975), 98, 100.

N26 Untermeyer, Louis. *The Pursuit of Poetry*. New York: Simon and Schuster, 1969, p. 203, 283.

N27 Vincent, Howard P. *The Tailoring of Melville's* White Jacket. Evanston, Ill.: Northwestern University Press, 1970, p. 211.
Quotes six lines of "The Unbeliever."

N28 Weiss, T., and Renée Weiss, eds. *Quarterly Review of Literature*, 7 (1953), 171.
The footnote mentions that the papers in this issue resulted from a conference on "Experimental and Formal Verse" at Bard College, no year given. Bishop is listed as having been one of the participants.

N29 Wilson, Edmund. "An Interview with Edmund Wilson." *New Yorker*, 38 (June 2, 1962), 128. Reprinted in *The Bit between My Teeth* (New York: Farrar, Straus and Giroux, 1965), p. 548.

O

Poems about or Dedicated

to Elizabeth Bishop

O1 Bernlef, J. "Elizabeth Bishop." *Het ontplofte gedicht* Over poëzie. Amsterdam, Em. Querido's Uitgeverij B.V., 1978, p. 78.

O2 Berryman, John. "Dream Song [187]." *Atlantic*, 221 (February 1968), 68. Reprinted in *His Toy, His Dream, His Rest: 308 Dream Songs.* (New York: Farrar, Straus and Giroux, 1968), p. 116, and *The Dream Songs* (New York: Farrar, Straus and Giroux, 1969), p. 206.

O3 Berryman, John. "Relations." *Love & Fame*. New York: Farrar, Straus and Giroux, 1970, p. 58.

O4 Berryman, John. "Dante's Tomb." *Love & Fame*. New York: Farrar, Straus and Giroux, 1970, p. 71.

O5 Lowell, Robert. "Skunk Hour (for Elizabeth Bishop)" (dedication). *Life Studies*. New York: Farrar, Straus and Cudahy, 1959, p. 89.

O6 Lowell, Robert. "For Elizabeth Bishop" (dedication). *Imitations*. New York: Farrar, Straus and Giroux, 1961, p. xv.

O7 Lowell, Robert. "The Scream (Derived from Elizabeth Bishop's Story, 'In the Village')." *Kenyon Review*, 24 (Autumn 1962), 624. Reprinted in *For the Union Dead*. New York: Farrar, Straus and Giroux, 1964, p. 8.

O8 Lowell, Robert. "Four Poems for Elizabeth Bishop: 1 Water 1948, 2 Flying from Bangor to Rio 1957, 3 Letter with Poems for a Letter with Poems, 4 Calling 1970." *Notebook*. New York: Farrar, Straus and Giroux, 1970, p. 234.

O9   Lowell, Robert. "For Elizabeth Bishop (Twenty-five Years) I. Water." *History*. New York: Farrar, Straus and Giroux, 1973, p. 196.

O10   Lowell, Robert. "For Elizabeth Bishop 2. Castine Maine." *History*. New York: Farrar, Straus and Giroux, 1973, p. 197.

O11   Lowell, Robert. "For Elizabeth Bishop 3. Letter with Poems for Letter with Poems." *History*. New York: Farrar, Straus and Giroux, 1973, p. 197.

O12   Lowell, Robert. "For Elizabeth Bishop 4." *History*. New York: Farrar, Straus and Giroux, 1973, p. 198.

O13   Lowell, Robert. "Water." *Selected Poems*. New York: Farrar, Straus and Giroux, 1976, p. 99.

O14   Lowell, Robert. "Thanks-Offering for Recovery." *Day by Day*. New York: Farrar, Straus and Giroux, 1977, p. 126.
"I give thanks, thanks— / thanks too for this small / Brazilian *ex voto*, this primitive head / sent me across the Atlantic by my friend. . . ."

O15   Macdonald, Cynthia. "Mutations: For Elizabeth Bishop and Robert Lowell" (dedication). *Pruning the Annuals*. West Hartford, Conn.: Bartholomew's Cobble, [1976], p. [12].

O16   Merrill, James. "The Victor Dog: For Elizabeth Bishop." *Braving the Elements*. New York: Atheneum, 1973, p. 70.

O17   Moss, Howard. "Letter to an Imaginary Brazil: For Elizabeth Bishop." *Selected Poems*. New York: Atheneum, 1973, p. 38.

O18   Shaw, Robert B. "To James Atlas: On His Way to Brazil." *Comforting the Wilderness*. Middletown, Conn.: Wesleyan University Press, 1977, p. 44.

O19   Strand, Mark. "The House in French Village: For Elizabeth Bishop." *New Yorker*, 53 (Oct. 10, 1977), 44. Reprinted in *The Late Hour* (New York: Atheneum, 1978), p. 38.

O20   Swenson, May. "Dear Elizabeth." *Half Sun Half Sleep*. New York: Charles Scribner's Sons, 1967, p. 39.

P

Anthologies Containing Work by Elizabeth Bishop

P1 *America Forever New*. Comp. Sara Brewton and John E. Brewton. New York: Thomas Y. Crowell Co., 1968.
Contains "The Imaginary Iceberg."

P2 *American Literature: The Makers and the Making*. Ed. Cleanth Brooks, R. W. B. Lewis, and Robert Penn Warren. New York: St. Martin's Press, 1973.
Contains "Filling Station," "Invitation to Miss Marianne Moore," "Letter to N.Y.," "Little Exercise," "Sunday, 4 A.M.," "Travelling in the Family."

P3 *American Poetry* (*American Literary Forms*). Ed. Karl Shapiro. New York: Thomas Y. Crowell Co., 1960.
Contains "A Miracle for Breakfast," "Wading at Wellfleet."

P4 *A Book of College Verse*. Ed. C. F. Main. Belmont, Calif.: Wadsworth Publishing Co., 1970.
Contains "Little Exercise."

P5 *Contemporary American Poets: American Poetry since 1940*. Ed. Mark Strand. New York: World Publishing Co., 1969.
Contains "At the Fishhouses," "First Death in Nova Scotia," "Visits to St. Elizabeths," "The Prodigal," "Little Exercise."

P6 *Crazy to Be Alive in Such a Strange World: Poems about People*. Selected by Nancy Larrick. New York: M. Evans and Co., 1977.
Contains "Manners."

P7 *The Criterion Book of Modern American Verse*. Ed. W. H. Auden. New York: Criterion Books, 1956.

Contains "From the Country to the City," "Little Exercise," "Roosters."

P8 *The Distinctive Voice.* Ed. William J. Martz. Glenview, Ill.: Scott, Foresman and Co., 1966.
Contains "The Armadillo," "Insomnia," "A Miracle for Breakfast," "Visits to St. Elizabeths," "Wading at Wellfleet."

P9 *Exploring Poetry.* Ed. M. L. Rosenthal and A. J. M. Smith. New York: Macmillan, 1955.
Contains "The Fish."

P10 *Fifteen Modern American Poets.* Ed. George Elliott. New York: Holt, Rinehart and Winston, 1962.
Contains "Arrival at Santos," "At the Fishhouses," "Cirque d'Hiver," "A Cold Spring," "The Fish," "A Miracle for Breakfast," "Over 2000 Illustrations and a Complete Concordance," "The Prodigal," "The Unbeliever," "View of the Capitol from the Library of Congress."

P11 *The Golden Journey: Poems for Young People.* Comp. Louise Bogan and William Jay Smith. Chicago: Reilly and Lee, 1965.
Contains "The Fish."

P12 *The Golden Treasury of Poetry.* Ed. Louis Untermeyer. Racine, Wis.: Golden Press, 1959.
Contains "The Fish."

P13 *How Does a Poem Mean?* 2d ed. Ed. John Ciardi and Miller Williams. Boston: Houghton Mifflin, 1975.
Contains "The Fish."

P14 *Invitation to Poetry: A Round of Poetry from John Skelton to Dylan Thomas.* Ed. Lloyd Frankenberg. New York: Doubleday and Co., 1956.
Contains "The Prodigal."

P15 *A Little Treasury of Love Poems.* Ed. John Holmes. New York: Charles Scribner's Sons, 1950.
Contains "Letter to N.Y."

P16 *The Looking Glass Book of Verse.* Comp. Janet Adam Smith. New York: Looking Glass Library, Random House, 1959.
Contains "The Map."

P17 *The Marvelous Light: Poets and Poetry.* Ed. Helen Plotz. New York: Thomas Y. Crowell Co., 1970.
Contains "Invitation to Miss Marianne Moore."

P18 *Modern American and British Poetry.* Ed. Louis Untermeyer, in consultation with Karl Shapiro and Richard Wilbur. New York: Harcourt, Brace and Co., 1955.

Contains "The Fish," "The Imaginary Iceberg," "Little Exercise," "The Man-Moth," "The Prodigal," "Seascape."

P19 *Modern American Poetry: Mid-Century Edition.* Ed. Louis Untermeyer. New York: Harcourt, Brace and Co., 1950.

Contains "The Fish," "The Imaginary Iceberg," "Little Exercise," "The Man-Moth."

P20 *Modern Poetry: American and British.* Ed. Kimon Friar and John Malcolm Brinnin. New York: Appleton-Century-Crofts, 1951.

Contains "The Monument," "The Weed."

P21 *Modern Verse in English, 1900–1950.* Ed. David Cecil and Allen Tate. New York: Macmillan, 1958.

Contains "At the Fishhouses," "The Imaginary Iceberg," "Invitation to Miss Marianne Moore."

P22 *The New Modern American and British Poetry.* Ed. Louis Untermeyer. New York: Harcourt, Brace and Co., 1950.

Contains "The Fish."

P23 *The New Modern Poetry.* Ed. M. L. Rosenthal. New York: Macmillan, 1967.

Contains "While Someone Telephones."

P24 *The New Pocket Anthology of American Verse from Colonial Days to the Present.* Ed. Oscar Williams. New York: World Publishing Co., 1955.

Contains "The Fish," "Roosters."

P25 The New Yorker *Book of Poems.* The Editors of *The New Yorker.* New York: Viking Press, 1969.

Contains "The Armadillo," "At the Fishhouses," "The Bight," "The Burglar of Babylon," "Filling Station," "First Death in Nova Scotia," "Large Bad Picture," "Little Exercise," "The Riverman," "Sandpiper," "Under the Window: Ouro Preto."

P26 *The Norton Anthology of Modern Poetry.* Ed. Richard Ellman and Robert O'Clair. New York: W. W. Norton, 1973.

Contains "The Armadillo," "Brazil, January 1, 1502," "The Fish," "The Man-Moth," "The Monument," "Over 2000 Illustrations and a Complete Concordance," "Seascape," "The Unbeliever."

P27 *100 American Poems of the Twentieth Century.* Ed. Laurence Perrine and James M. Reid. New York: Harcourt, Brace and World, 1966.

Contains "The Fish," "The Man-Moth."

P28 *100 Modern Poems*. Comp. Selden Rodman. New York: Pelegrini and Cudahy, 1949.
Contains "Roosters."

P29 *100 Post War Poems*. Ed. M. L. Rosenthal. New York: Macmillan, 1968.
Contains "Arrival at Santos."

P30 *The Penguin Book of American Verse*. Ed. Geoffrey Moore. London: Penguin Books, 1954.
Contains "The Man-Moth."

P31 *People in Poetry*. Ed. Marjorie B. Smiley. New York: Macmillan, 1969.
Contains "Jerónimo's House."

P32 *The Poem: A Critical Anthology*. Ed. Josephine Miles. Englewood Cliffs, N. J.: Prentice Hall, 1959.
Contains "A Cold Spring," "The Fish."

P33 *Poems and Poets*. Ed. David Aloian. New York: Webster Division, McGraw-Hill, 1965.
Contains "The Fish."

P34 *Poems of Doubt and Belief: An Anthology of Modern Religious Poetry*. Ed. Tom F. Driver and Robert Pack. New York: Macmillan, 1964
Contains "Over 2000 Illustrations and a Complete Concordance."

P35 *Poems on Poetry: The Mirror's Garland*. Ed. Robert Wallace and James G. Taaffe. New York: E. P. Dutton, 1965.
Contains "The Monument."

P36 *Poems to Read Aloud*. Ed. Edward Hodnett. New York: W. W. Norton, 1967.
Contains "At the Fishhouses."

P37 *Poetry: An Introductory Anthology*. Ed. Hazard Adams. Boston: Little, Brown and Co., 1968.
Contains "The Fish."

P38 *Poetry for Pleasure: The Hallmark Book of Poetry*. New York: Doubleday, 1960.
Contains "The Fish," "Late Air."

P39 *Poetry in English*. Ed. Warren Taylor and Donald Hall. New York: Macmillan, 1963, 1970.
Contains "The Monument."

P40 *The Poetry of the Negro, 1749–1970*. Ed. Langston Hughes and Arna Botemps. New York: Doubleday, 1949, 1970.
Contains "Songs for a Colored Singer."

P41 *A Poetry Sampler.* Ed. Donald Hall. New York: Franklin Watts, 1962.
Contains "The Bight."

P42 *The Poet's Story.* Ed. Howard Moss. New York: Macmillan, 1973.
Contains "In Prison."

P43 *Reading Modern Poetry.* Ed. Paul Engle and Warren Carrier. Key Editions. Glenview, Ill.: Scott, Foresman and Co., 1955.
Contains "The Imaginary Iceberg," "The Map."

P44 *The Reading of Poetry.* Ed. William Sheldon, Nellie Lyons, and Polly Roualt. Boston: Allyn and Bacon, 1963.
Contains "A Miracle for Breakfast."

P45 *The Silver Swan.* Ed. Horace Gregory and Marya Zaturenska. New York: Macmillan, Collier Books, 1968.
Contains "Casabianca."

P46 *Studying Poetry: A Critical Anthology of English and American Poems.* Ed. Karl Broeber and John O. Lyons. New York: Harper and Row, 1965.
Contains "A Cold Spring," "A Miracle for Breakfast."

P47 *Translations by American Poets.* Ed. Jean Garrigue. Athens: Ohio University Press, 1970.
Contains "Travelling in the Family," "From *The Death and Life of a Severino.*"

P48 *A Treasury of Great Poems, English and American.* Ed. Louis Untermeyer. New York: Simon and Schuster, 1955.
Contains "The Fish."

P49 *Twentieth-Century American Poetry.* Ed. Conrad Aiken. New York: Modern Library, 1963.
Contains "The Fish," "Invitation to Miss Marianne Moore."

P50 *Twentieth Century Poetry: American and British (1900–1970).* Ed. John Malcolm Brinnin and Bill Read. New York: McGraw-Hill, 1963, 1970.
Contains "A Cold Spring," "Florida," "Letter to N.Y.," "The Prodigal."

P51 *Understanding Poetry.* Ed. Cleanth Brooks and Robert Penn Warren. New York: Holt, Rinehart and Winston, 1960.
Contains "Little Exercise."

P52 *The Viking Book of Poetry of the English Speaking World.* Ed. Richard Aldington. New York: Viking Press, 1959.
Contains "The Fish."

P53 *The Voice That Is Great within Us*. Ed. Hayden Carruth. New York: Bantam, 1970.
Contains "The Armadillo," "Visits to St. Elizabeths."
P54 *The Wind Is Round*. Comp. Sara Hannum and John Terry Chase. New York: Atheneum, 1970.
Contains "Electrical Storm."

Q

Interviews

Q1 Léo Gilson Ribeiro. "Elisabeth Bishop: A Poetisa, O Cajú e Mi-cuçu." *Correiro de Manhã* (Rio de Janeiro), Dec. 13, 1964, p. 16.

Q2 Ashley Brown. "An Interview with Elizabeth Bishop." *Shenandoah*, 17 (Winter 1966), 3. J4.

Q3 "Ouro Prêto: primavera no Festival de Inverno." *Visão* (São Paulo, Brazil), 35 (Aug. 1, 1969), 50.

Q4 Regina Colônia. "Elizabeth Bishop: A Poesia como 'Way of Life.' " *Jornal do Brasil* (Rio de Janeiro), June 6, 1970, p. 8.

Q5 Eileen Farley. "Roethke Called Her a 'Quick Kid in a Caper.' " *University of Washington Daily* (Seattle), May 28, 1974, p. 14.

Q6 Anna Quindlen. "Elizabeth Bishop." *New York Post*, April 3, 1976, p. 33.

Q7 Jim Bross. "Reading 'Scares' Poet Bishop." *Norman* (Oklahoma) *Transcript*, April 11, 1976, p. 1.

√ Q8 Leslie Hanscom. "A Poet Who Doesn't Wear Her Woes on Her Sleeve." *Newsday*, Feb. 6, 1977, p. Ideas / 18.

Q9 Beatriz Schiller. "Elizabeth Bishop: A Poesia Que Nasceu do Sofrimento." *Revista do Domingo, Jornal do Brasil* (Rio de Janeiro), May 8, 1977, pp. 22–25.

Q10 "David W. McCullough's Eye on Books." *Book-of-the-Month Club News*, May 1977, p. 6.

√Q11 George Starbuck. " 'The Work!' A Conversation with Elizabeth Bishop." *Ploughshares*, 3, nos. 3 and 4 (1977), 11. J30.

√Q12 Alexandra Johnson. "Artists and Their Inspiration: Poet Elizabeth Bishop: Geography of the Imagination." *Christian Science Monitor*, 70 (March 23, 1978), 24.

Q13 J. Bernlef. *Het ontplofte gedicht* Over poëzie. Amsterdam: Em. Querido's Uitgeverij B.V., 1978, pp. 84–92.

Q14 Sheila Hale. "Woman Writers in America: A. S. Byatt Examines the Contribution of Women Writers to the American Literary Tradition and Sheila Hale Talks to Ten of the Most Important in America Today." *Harpers and Queen*, July 1978, pp. 59–61. J5.

Q15 Elizabeth Spires. "An Afternoon with Elizabeth Bishop." *Vassar Quarterly*, 75 (Winter 1979), 4–9.

R

Published Letters and Excerpts from Letters

R1 Excerpt from a letter. "Inchiesta su Ezra Pound e La Poesia Americana." (anonymous article contains a previously unpublished quotation about Ezra Pound by EB in Italian). *Nuova Corriente: rivistas di letteratura*, 5–6 (1956), 205.

R2 Excerpt from a letter to Anne Stevenson. Anne Stevenson. *Elizabeth Bishop*. New York: Twayne Publishers, 1966, p. 66.

R3 Letter to the editor. "Unamerican Editions." *Times Literary Supplement*, Feb. 15, 1968, p. 157. **K7c**.

R4 Letter to the editor. *Kayak*, 19 (August 1969), 50.

R5 Letter to the editor. *The Little Magazine*, 5 (Fall 1971/Winter 1972), 79.

R6 Letter to Mr. Kaplan. *Pourboire 16: Peter Kaplan's Book*. Ed. Jaimy Gordon and Ray Ragosta. Providence: Pourboire Press, 1978, p. 39.

S

Obituaries

S1   Tony Schwartz. "Elizabeth Bishop Is Dead at 68; Won Pulitzer for Poetry in 1956." *New York Times*, Oct. 8, 1979, p. B13.

S2   "Elizabeth Bishop, Poet, Dies; Lectured at Harvard 7 Years." *Harvard Crimson*, Oct. 9, 1979, pp. 1, 6.
Contains statements by Lloyd Schwartz, David Ferry, and Alan Williamson.

S3   [Martin Hightower]. "Elizabeth Bishop, Noted Poet, Dies." *Harvard Gazette*, Oct. 12, 1979, pp. 1, 2.
Contains statements by Robert Fitzgerald and Alan Williamson.

S4   Robert Taylor. "Book-Making." *Boston Globe*, Oct. 14, 1979, p. C2.
Contains Lloyd Schwartz's statement made at Sanders Theatre, Oct. 7, 1979.

S5   Lloyd Schwartz. "Elizabeth Bishop, 1911–1979." *Boston Phoenix*, Oct. 16, 1979, p. 12.

S6   Peggy Rizza. "Elizabeth Bishop (1911–1979)." *The Real Paper*, Oct. 20, 1979, p. 38.

S7   "Transition." *Newsweek*, 94 (Oct. 22, 1979), 72.

S8   "Milestones." *Time*, 114 (Oct. 22, 1979), 105.

S9   Robert Pinsky. "Elizabeth Bishop, 1911–1979." *New Republic*, 181 (Nov. 10, 1979), 32–33.

S10   James Merrill. "Elizabeth Bishop (1911–1979)." *New York Review of Books*, 26 (Dec. 6, 1979), 6.

T

Addenda

T1 *A Library of Literary Criticism: Modern American Literature*, vol. 4, Supplement (ALLC). Dorothy Nyren Curley, Coordinator. New York: Frederick Ungar Publishing Co., 1969 [1973], pp. 54–55. Abstracts of **K7f, K9u, K9m, K9v**.

T2 Alfred Kazin. Review of *The Survivor*, by Terrence Des Pres. *New York Times Book Review*, March 14, 1976, p. 1. "In our 'worst century so far,' as Elizabeth Bishop once put it" (first sentence, second paragraph), from the dust jacket for *Life Studies*. (**N**)

T3 Anne Hussey. "For E.B." (dedication). *Baddeck & Other Poems*. Middletown, Conn.: Wesleyan University Press, 1978, p. 5. (**O**)

T4 *Contemporary Literary Criticism*, vol. 9 (CLC 9). Ed. Dedria Bryfonski. Detroit: Gale Research Co., 1978, pp. 88–98. Contains abstracts of **J21**; **H1**: Ashbery, Paz, Mortimer, Vendler, Moss, Schwartz, Estess; **K11gg; J24**.

T5 Ernest Stefanik. "Elizabeth Bishop 1911–." *First Printings of American Authors: Contributions toward Descriptive Checklists*, vol. 2. Ed. Matthew Bruccoli. Detroit: Gale Research Co., 1978, pp. 43–44. Note: *Poems: North & South—A Cold Spring* was *not* republished as *Poems*, Chatto and Windus.

T6 Sybil Estess. "Bishop, Elizabeth." *American Women Writers: A Critical Reference Guide from Colonial Times to the Present in Four Volumes*, vol. 1: A to E. Ed. Lina Mainiero. New York: Frederick Ungar Publishing Co., 1979, pp. 156–162. (**I**)

T7 Ivar Ivask. "Elizabeth Bishop: 1976 Laureate of the Books Abroad / Neustadt International Prize." *Books Abroad*, 50 (Spring 1976), 263–265. (**M**)

T8 Mary McCarthy. "In Her Own Words: A New Kind of McCarthyism: Actor Kevin Interviews Sister Mary on Her Books, Loves & Life." *People*, 12 (Nov. 12, 1979), 99. (**N**)

T9 *A Little Treasury of Modern Poetry: English and American.* Ed. Oscar Williams. London: Routledge, Kegan Paul Ltd., 1948. (P) Contains "Roosters," "The Imaginary Iceberg."

T10 Lloyd Schwartz. "Elizabeth Bishop." *Ploughshares*, 5, no. 4 (1979), 172–173.

Appendix I   *Unpublished Poems*

App. 1 "Brittania Rules the Waves." Unpublished. Original date unknown. Pinned to a letter to Marianne Moore dated April 13, 1935. Rosenbach Museum collection, Philadelphia.

App. 2 "Lullabye for the Cat." Unpublished. Typed on an undated page but referred to in a letter to Marianne Moore dated November 24, 1937. Sent without a covering letter in an envelope postmarked 5 November 1937. Rosenbach Museum collection, Philadelphia.

App. 3 "To Be Written on the Mirror in Whitewash." Unpublished. Typed on the same page as "Lullabye for the Cat," which is referred to in a letter to Marianne Moore dated November 24, 1937. Sent without a covering letter in an envelope postmarked 5 November 1937. Rosenbach Museum collection, Philadelphia.

App. 4 "Sunday at Key West." Unpublished. In a letter to Marianne Moore dated February 14, 1938. Rosenbach Museum collection, Philadelphia.

App. 5 "Pleasure Seas." Unpublished. Sold to *Harper's Bazaar* in 1940. Never printed. Miss Bishop has the only copy known to exist.

App. 6 "The Fanny Farmer Cookbook." Unpublished. Written to Frank Bidart on the flyleaf of *The Fanny Farmer Cookbook*, Christmas 1971. Collection of Frank Bidart.

Appendix II *Unauthorized Printing*

App. II *THE FISH.* [1974] (first edition, first impression)

THE FISH | Elizabeth Bishop

Collation: broadside.

Contents: recto: EB's poem "The Fish" printed vertically in three columns, signed by EB in the space between her name and the printed text, verso numbered in pencil, '8/12', lower left corner.

Typography: 12 pt. Intertype Garamond, Garamond no. 3.

Paper: 14⅞ × 10 in. (377 × 254 mm.); unglazed, yWhite (Centroid 92) wove paper; all edges trimmed.

Publication: 13 copies of this broadside were printed for Mr. David Ishii, bookseller and fisherman, by a private printer, John and Karen Sollid,

Seattle, Washington, approximately one month before EB's arrival for the Roethke Memorial Reading in May 1974. During her stay, EB signed 12 copies. Seven copies were distributed; five remain in the possession of Mr. Ishii. One unsigned copy belongs to the printer. None are for sale.

Index